CONTEMPORARY FINNISH POETRY

Herbert Lomas is a freelance poet, critic and translator, and a former lecturer at the universities of Helsinki and London. He is a regular critic for *London Magazine*, as well as other journals. He has worked for many years for the quarterly *Books in Finland* and in 1981 published a highly praised anthology of Finnish poetry and prose in translation, *Territorial Song* (London Magazine Editions). His most recent poetry collections are *Public Footpath* (Anvil Press, 1981), *Fire in the Garden* (Oxford University Press, 1984) and *Letters in the Dark* (Oxford University Press, 1986). He lives in Aldeburgh, Suffolk.

CONTEMPORARY FINNISH POETRY

EDITED & TRANSLATED BY

Herbert Lomas

BLOODAXE BOOKS

ISBN: 1 85224 147 0

First published 1991 by
Bloodaxe Books Ltd,
P.O. Box 1SN,
Newcastle upon Tyne NE99 1SN.

This book is published with the financial support
of the Arts Council of Great Britain.

Bloodaxe Books Ltd also acknowledges
the financial assistance of Northern Arts.

Typesetting by Bryan Williamson, Darwen, Lancashire.

Arts Council Funded

Printed in Great Britain by
Bell & Bain Limited, Glasgow, Scotland.

Every house has many builders
and is never finished

PAAVO HAAVIKKO

Acknowledgements

My indebtedness is enormous. Many thanks are due to the Chairman, Editor and Editorial Board of *Books from Finland*, where many of the poems first appeared and to the Finnish Literature Information Centre, whose staff did all in their power to make my research and visits productive, culturally instructive and enjoyable.

I must also thank the poets for their indulgence and must apologise to the many distinguished poets I have not been able to find space for, regretfully, and for a variety of reasons, including untranslatability, or my own inadequacy.

Acknowledgements and thanks are also due to the Arts Council of Great Britain for providing a translation grant for this anthology, and to the following for permission to publish these translations of work by Finnish writers, and for the photographs: Art House (for Paavo Haavikko); Mia Berner (Pentti Saarikoski); Otava (Tuomas Anhava, Jarkko Laine, Hannu Mäkelä, Lassi Nummi, Caj Westerberg); Tammi (Väinö Kirstinä, Eeva-Liisa Manner, Eira Stenberg, Sirkka Turkka); Werner Söderström Osakeyhtiö (Risto Ahti, Pentti Holappa, Eila Kivikk'aho, Kirsi Kunnas, Aila Meriluoto, Mirkka Rekola, Pentti Saaritsa, Satu Salminiitty, Ilpo Tiihonen). Copyright dates for poems are as given after book titles at the head of each selection from those books. The cover photograph of Taivalköngäs by Tauno Kohonen is reproduced by kind permission of Luonnonkuva-Arkisto, Helsinki.

Contents

Introduction

I.

Finnish poetry is a popular poetry. Without talking down, or lowering standards, at times being quite demanding, it claims readers because they feel they need it.

It is neither a cult, an academic preserve, nor a tradition surviving on mere momentum. It does not solve problems, or try to, but people do turn to it for solace, inspiration, stimulation to think about themselves, extension of experience and the shaping spirit. This poetry has fed a clearly felt hunger in the Finnish public: the need, not only for art, but for companionable reports on what it is like to be a Finn in this phase of the muddle for survival. But like all authentic localised reports, its appeal is universal.

It is very spare. Our poetry can look baroque to the Finns, not leaving enough silence between the words. Nevertheless, the poetry is not all of one sort, and one can find rhetoric and baroque extension here too. The younger poets are already moving in new directions, moralising and deploying chromatic speech. Inheriting a flexible common idiom forged by the previous generation, they have been liberated.

Why has this new experiment worked so well? Till the War this non-Indo-European language had perhaps become too stiff-collared in forms borrowed from Teutonic languages. The new idiom was a *native* idiom – even though a lot of models were sought in America, Sweden and Japan – closer to the rhythms of the ancient poetry. Finnish has a highly vocalic polysyllabic front-stressed vocabulary, inflected with thirteen cases and capable of a labyrinthine syntax. Very close to Estonian and some Ugrian offshoots, distantly related to Hungarian, it has otherwise no resemblance to any other European language. The loosening of form enabled poets to rediscover Finnish rhythms – and with them Finnish reverie.

'Modernism' – not quite modernism as we have known it in England – came late to Finland as the prevailing style, though something resembling it had paid earlier visits. It was reinvented in an exciting, indigenous and accessible form by those who had been children during the long, snowy, hungry, gruelling wars, first against Hitler's ally Stalin, then, by one of those ironies of war, against Britain and America's ally Stalin, and finally against Hitler's Germany.

Paavo Haavikko and **Pentti Saarikoski** became the most famous of the brilliant generation of twenty-year-olds who led the rejuvenation of Finnish poetry in the 1950s. Saarikoski died in 1983, at forty-five, and Haavikko achieved a high degree of international recognition in 1984, at fifty-three, when he won the prestigious Neustadt International Prize for Literature. Thus, thirty years from its start, and when, no doubt, some new direction is already germinating, this is a good moment to observe what has been happening.

Haavikko and Saarikoski, born six years apart, were the most controversial poets in a critical generation, well-read, bristling to the high-speed second industrial revolution forced on them by war reparations. They were historically conscious, aware of being potentially dead water between two tides of world power, and replete with imagery imbibed with their mothers' milk: the frozen corpses of a hundred thousand young Finns, perhaps twelve or thirteen per cent of the country's younger men; the long border with the nervous Soviet Union; the loss of Karelia and the arrival of its refugees; the fires and the near-starvation; the precarious political balance; the country's uneasy neutral position outside the Soviet Bloc, and the diplomacy needed to maintain it; the pulping and processing of Finland's economy, and its concept of its identity. The poets grabbed what they needed from modernist techniques and created an original and popular way of articulating disjunction, doubt, determination to survive, and aesthetic excitement, in a world not very interested in the individuality of small countries.

The poems thrilled the young because they publicised their conflicts obliquely or directly in new and arresting art-forms, making sense of the emerging sensibility that, to war-reparation-weary parents, could seem a flamboyant leg-pull. The movement was an adaptation and a new kind of maturity, a fresh confrontation of fresh reality, and the poets were not to be browbeaten by the craggy agonies and achievements of an heroic but sometimes humourless war generation. Saarikoski was born two years before 1939 in Karelia, now annexed to the Soviet Union, its Finnish population exiled to other parts of Finland. In 1962, surrounded by the confusing international political signals, looking at Finland's precarious neutrality, apparently balanced on diplomatic tact, Saarikoski wrote:

> This began two years before the wars in
> a village that now belongs to the Soviet Union
> my sole recollection of the war is the fires they were great
> they don't come like that nowadays
> I run to the window at the wail of the fire engine
> I was on the move all my childhood
> I turned communist
> I went into the cemetery and studied the angels
> they don't come like that nowadays –

sella in curuli struma Nonius sedet
I burned books in Alexandria
I played the part of a stone and a flower and built a church
I wrote poems to myself myself the chair went up and down
high-backed ones like that don't come nowadays
high poetry there is I'm expecting a cheque
  Which is the mistake, the wrong way, or the right, not the Way
  it's ±2
I live the future times
I read tomorrow's newspapers
I support Khrushchev carry the owl from room to room
I'm looking for the right place for it, This began

In an ironical experiment with the prosaic, he summed up the resignation of the fifties:

I live in Helsinki
Helsinki is the capital of Finland.
It's situated by the sea 120 miles west of Leningrad.
Helsinki is an expanding city, and the rents are high.
We sit in the midst of our forests backs to the giant and watch
  his image in a well. He wears a dark suit a white shirt
and
  a silver tie. In his country everything's different,
  there they walk on their heads or without a head.
We sit in the midst of our own forests,
but far in the West there's a land with coastal waters bobbing
  with big eyes, and they can see this far.
Helsinki's being rebuilt after Alvar Aalto's plan.

Though not great poetry, or Saarikoski's best, this is an early, concise, humorous and ironical definition of a condition.

Finland's economy and morale have improved beyond recognition. She has a flourish and a style that would have seemed out of reach in 1951, when Haavikko at twenty published his first volume, and still in 1958 when Saarikoski published his at twenty-one. Yet even in the 1970s, in the already embellished new capitalist economy, with its pleasurable consensus of old and new architecture, its executive restaurants, stylish clothes, and elegant shop windows, Claes Andersson, a Swedish-speaking Finn, could consciously echo Saarikoski in a new definition of the collective muffling of personality:

In Helsinki the houses haven't any special beauty
You won't find any special shadiness in the parks
The air's no smoggier than in other great cities
The people are no better off than somewhere else
Helsinki's a city without a face, with
  a smiling facelessness seaward
The whole city's mostly back of the head and neck, or back
Just now and then you might think you can see a smile

starting in the wrinkles of the neck, a laugh in its back
Then desperately you go scooting round and round
trying for a sighting of its eyes, its mouth
And then the city hunches and huddles into itself, draws
the mist closer round its shoulders
You can love Helsinki for its piddlingness, for its
lack of a distinct face, its insensibility
to those who fall down in the streets
and go on lying there

The back is to the sea now, but the poem ironically defines the continued undesirability of insularity, personal or national.

II.

Modernism was not entirely new to Finland. **Aaro Hellaakoski** (1893-1952) had, influenced by cubism and Apollinaire, invented some experimental poems in the 1920s, before reverting to more traditional metres.

He was clearly trying to get 'the rhythm of the internal combustion engine' into a poem like this:

9 p.m.
evening street scurry
with a gloss of cobblestones
your path home under the line of streetlamps
is a gaudy fiction
when happy hurry
you come back melodious din
from work a mannequin's
misted smile
radiant window displays
thousands of strange walkers
car paws
are clawing
the street
eyefulls
light torrents into your head
a white glove
STOP
A WHITE GLOVE ON AN OUTSTRETCHED HAND
hrr-rr-rh
cross safely ready-for-bed man
on your evening evening way
windows and windows are blazing
your thoughts are already relishing sleep
sweet sweet tired-out feeling
eager evening loveliness
dolce far niente

This is an interesting experiment, yet I think he was wise not to go on with the style. For me there is more pleasure in the following poem – typical of his later style; and it seems closer, not only to his more authentic poetic sensibility, but, curiously enough, to many of the modernist poems in this volume – though now I have in mind other poets than Haavikko and Saarikoski:

Message

Quiescent waterstretch
split by a splash.

Mysteryfish
swished back in a splash.

Depth message fetched
in a moment of flash
splashed on the waterstretch.

Wish I knew that fish.

The implication is clear. In his urban poem he was close to his current experience, but the experience was not close to his heart. In 'Message' he was being true to the kind of moment that moved not only him but his fellow Finns and the later poets – a kind of moment the tribe had been experiencing for thousands of years and is still experiencing. Even in the following more obviously metrical piece one can see the kind of experience that moves, say, Eeva-Liisa Manner:

Under the sleeping branches, light
glimmers oddly in the night.

Through the wood the cryptic road
comes from nowhere, nowhere goes.

My shadow left me. Very soon
my body too dissolved in moon

My footfall hovers ownerless.
My fingers touch on emptiness.

Perhaps the most accomplished poet of his generation, alive, as most educated Finns wish to be, to what was going on abroad, Hellaakoski developed from a critical and egocentric commentator into an evocator of mystical dissolution and tenderly erotic love:

Hours of midnight tiptoed by
two touching in their slumbering.

Quiet hand sought quiet hand
with unimpassioned questioning.

Close-pressed to interrogate
the vein's pulsation at your throat,

Words, I found them, many, many
for each shift of limb, each mote.

Through our bodies crept the hours
sensitively, light of foot.

My thinking drifted backwards, forwards,
with the warming of its mood.

Don't you feel our nightflight wasn't
quite in vain, or meanly flown?

Did I somewhere brush, so softly,
lands of sleep you walk alone?

One can see here an authentic Finnish sensibility working within a rhythm and a stanza derived from other cultures. In studying foreign models the best recent poets have not lost their Finnish sensibility and seem to have arrived at a shape closer to Finnish rhythms. Caj Westerberg, for instance, is carefully attendant to those evanescent awarenesses and suggestions of communion with nature, or dissolution within it:

The lake settles into the night
without a shiver:
a forest mirror sucking the sky deep in.
A lone-flying woodcock
pencils a *frisson* of shadow on the water's skin.
Your skin
shudders now.

At the same time he does not ignore the imagery and the pressures of the "real world" of economics, urban struggle and adaptation. These, and their meaning, are often hinted at obliquely, but sometimes quite directly too:

Buying and selling
selling and buying
our own life.
Bad, bad.
It's dear,
and it's going cheap.

Romance has to live as best it can:

I look out of a bus window in a light mist and a slight snow:
let's hope a craving for ecstasy will be fed by
that stack of coal on the wharf:
the poor man's Kilimanjaro.

Trams are certainly as prominent as in Väinö Kirstinä:

. . . a tram pulls up, stops, opens its throat
and bares its teeth.
Then the jaws clack shut and the whole contraption
slides off.

In the maple
there's a convulsion.

Hellaakoski definitely seems to suggest guidelines, possibilities and problems, and it is not surprising that he was respected by the young poets emerging in the 1950s, and that he in turn followed and supported them.

Hellaakoski was not, of course, alone in the 1920s. 'The Torch Bearers', for instance, wrote non-rhyming free verse – with an emotional response to exotic lands and 'the romance of the machine'. Their impetus was not lasting, however, and they left little after-image. Some of them, however, like P. Mustapää, who gave up poetry during the 1930s to concentrate on research as a Professor of Folklore, made a return of a different kind and produced a new fertilisation in the post-war resurgence.

Another forerunner was **Edith Södergran**, who appeared as a poet in 1916, in the same year as Hellaakoski. She belonged to the Swedish-speaking minority in Finland (then about ten per cent of the population) and was the most prominent of several modernists among them. They differed considerably from each other in both ideas and temperament, but they were the first Scandinavian *avant-garde* and have remained influential.

Södergran achieved recognition throughout Scandinavia after her death and continues to be revered. Her short tuberculosis-ridden life and blazing personality are no doubt partly responsible for this, but she is studied as a poet of ideas and passion. She was an experimenter with free forms and was to some extent an imagist – contemporary with American imagism – but she did not wish to innovate to the borders of intelligibility, or even absurdity, as Haavikko and Saarikoski sometimes do. On the contrary she wanted her passions to emerge with the utmost clarity and subdue the hearts and minds of her readers with expressionist force. She is closer to, say, the D.H. Lawrence of *Look, We Have Come Through* than to Eliot or Pound. Her social themes are pursued, not politically or directly, but prophetically, envisaging a new order of saints, mystical poets, artists and sages. Nothing could be further from the severe nihilism of Haavikko or the materialism-fading-into-agnosticism of Saarikoski:

People are poorly acquainted with themselves
and suppose they're as beggared as they seem,
ignorant that the gods are alive incognito in their breasts.
The gods laugh. Life is theirs.
They drive a chariot harnessed with fire,
and in it a queen – too superb
to be named in anything but whispers.

Kneel. The gods are coming.
The gods are resurrecting from dusty brows,
lifting all the world to their own altitudes.

She has her own style of morbidity too, a personal experience, but generalised into a definition of the human condition, particularly the feminine condition. It becomes the starting point for conflicting impulses towards the Nietzschian superman and esoteric Christianity. In feeling she is thus a late romantic, moving like Strindberg between the poles of assertion and submission, euphoria and death-longing, with a near-arrogant conviction of prophetic vocation, her disillusion unstained by cynicism.

Yet her rhetoric is a notation of lived experiences, inspiring or wounding moments:

My soul was a blue dress, sky-blue:
I left it on a rock beside the sea
and came to you naked, a woman.
As a woman I dined at your table
and drank a goblet of wine and breathed in roses.
You thought I was lovely – someone seen in a dream.

I forgot it all – my childhood, my homeland –
knew nothing but the captivity of your caresses.
And you smiled and took a looking-glass
and told me to look.
I saw my shoulders crumbling to dust.
I saw my beauty sick – its one will, to vanish.
Oh, hold me close in your arms, so tight I'll not need a thing.

The cooler poets of this volume – cooler not in disturbance but understatement – have avoided this directness, while learning from her free rhythms, her blend of the literary and the colloquial, her expansion of subject matter and to some extent her poetic formulae. She often imagines life at some fantasy court, for instance:

And the queen asked her confidential counsellor,
'Who's this wicked woman my husband's in love with?'
'He loves any woman who sets his blood on fire.'
'But who's the one I must fight hardest with?'
'It's your own black rage you must fight hardest with.'
'But how can I fight my own black rage?'
'Let the courier kiss you when he comes at sundown.'

The touch is lighter here than usual, but a comparison with Tuomas Anhava shows the ironic distance travelled:

Once upon a time there wasn't a kingdom that didn't have a king and he didn't have a head.

It weighed heavily on him.

And he sought out a man who didn't have a spine and placed his head on the man's shoulders.

> The king didn't die. Long live the king.
> And he lived happily ever after, and the kingdom endured for a thousand years and wasn't once upon a time.

However distanced, Södergran's poem is about herself, and her poems are usually more obviously so. Anhava's is about – what? Constitutional monarchy, moral failure, confusion, evasion, mankind's abdication, the escape from responsibility? Or is the main point the poetic game? Though it combines satire with surrealism, it has the impersonality of a fairy tale. Södergran's fairy tales do not have the impersonality of fairy tales.

Haavikko's early poetry is centred on imaginary landscapes that often resemble Södergran's:

> And I ride through charted lands,
> but the fowling hawks are being freed,
> and I ride forward crouching,
> cape flapping,
> riding ahead of the squadrons threatening their king,
> across fords and slopes,
> hooves drumming under myriadmorphic trees:
> I must ride from night into night
> swifter than the squadrons of thought,
> squander myself responding to the fullness of days
> or throw in my hand.

That could easily be by Södergran. The later Haavikko moves from dreamy landscape to a sometimes angry pseudo-objectivity, but surrealistic locales remain. In the following, for example, can we not see Södergran's court filtered through Anhava?

> My grandfather, the Emperor, was, as you know, mad,
> wrote poems in the presence of others.
> You want war,
> it's available.
> You walk stiff-legged,
> like soldiers do, hysterics before an attack.
> Hysteria is an illness that never gets better.
> The hysteric is a winner, he never gives in.
> No use my talking. I'll read his poem:
>
> The mist is so dense, the water's hidden from the bridge.
> The flowers are having fits,
> as they have
> to die so nonsensically.

It seems obvious that Haavikko must have studied Södergran. His phrase in *Winter Palace* 'seutu joka ei ole paikka' – literally 'a region that is not a place' – is suspiciously like the title of Södergran's posthumous volume *Landet Som Icke Är* ('The Land That Is Not'). So much so that I have appropriated 'the land that is not' to translate the difficult Finnish phrase, less literally than usual. I find it difficult to believe that the allusion is not conscious; but Haavikko has given the phrase a semiotic emphasis. Whereas Södergran implies a place that *is*, after all, Haavikko uses the allusion to underline the deceptive power of words: the power of words to suggest that something that does not exist does exist. The words of a poem can only invent: they cannot, Haavikko is telling us, in parable after parable in *Winter Palace*, invent reality. Even the persona of the poet and his locale are fantasy-inventions.

Saarikoski, too, in his first book, shows a detectable touch of Södergran:

> The grey days wandered by with drooping heads.
> He didn't turn, the shadows paled,
> the days stretched away.
> His wings grew in the nights, and he wrote the songs over the water.

Is this uncharacteristic poem directly influenced, or are we dealing with something endemic in the Finnish consciousness? At any rate, Saarikoski had soon extirpated anything like this, and was correcting romantic classicism with a harder-eyed classicism of his own. His poem on Dionysus is surely a deliberate parody. Here is Södergran:

> O Dionysus, you come along with the sun's horses
> from the far reaches of space.
> The earth is hot with tears, a woman waiting, at prayer.
> O Dionysus, Dionysus!
> Over our heads we hear the thunder of your horses.
> It's freedom, freedom the quick reins are singing.
> O Dionysus, Dionysus,
> I scramble onto your horses,
> grab the chariot wheels with crazy hands.
> The crazy are capable of anything.
> Like spring sun, I'm clambering into your chariot.
> Everywhere round, it's nothing but space blue with spring.
> Carolling birds are celebrating on earth –
> and just so your horses are galloping like a storm.
> All space is singing the resurrection.

Saarikoski addresses Dionysus as, not the god of resurrection, but senility. In 'Old Age' the dotard's resurrection is a vomit even after he has collapsed dead-drunk:

> Oh dear, Dionysus, gaga and doddering!
> Down on his knees in the park, hands trembling,
> and when his thyrsus snaps, the girls
> tumble out of their hidey-holes and twirl away giggling.
> Poor Dionysus!
> On his belly in the park, feet north,
> beard going green even in death,
> and stentorian as a whole city
> even in death,
> oh dear, Dionysus.

So much for the gods 'rising from dusty brows'. Yet the poem has its own compassion; it is not merely cynical. It is about man: not godlike, strong, a potential superman; but tragically vulnerable – the victim not only of old age, scorn, and the collapse of the flesh, but of his own weakness. This drunk is an outward and visible sign of everybody's inward capacity for failure, however kept at bay. He is the scapegoat: he bears the guilt as well as the suffering of 'the whole city' – more than any individual can bear or should be asked to bear. For me, therefore, the poem is not only wittier but infinitely more mature than Södergran's, in spite of its air of irresponsible frivolity.

III.

The other poets in the volume constitute a movement in the best sense: they are a family, rather than an organisation: influencing each other, but intensifying their individuality through that very influence.

Eeva-Liisa Manner began publishing in 1944, at twenty-three, but adapted her style to the new trends in the 50s; it does seem to have constituted not a move into the fashion but a self-discovery: this is what she was looking for.

She too is a visionary, but an exposed and unquiet one: 'It's easy to walk into Hades...but getting back is difficult' (facilis descensus Averno...sed revocare gradum...hoc opus, hic labor est): the allusion is thoroughly personalised, her fusion of the mythical, the private and the public seamless. She writes both poetry and prose, carefully distinguishing the two: 'Prose, let it be hard as you like, make you restless'; but 'Poetry's a letter from a distant country pushed under the door'...'so large and white it's filling the whole house'. The image recurs:

I thought it was a letter, thrown on the porch,
but it was only a gleam of moon.
I picked up the glow from the floor.
How light it was, the moon's letter,
and everything was sagging, like iron, over there.

It's as if her hand might go right through matter and touch something more luminous.

A jetty, and two steps down:
space is white.
Across what void?
Or not a drop at all?
Merely a lost lake,
and a swan's wake on the water?

Her metaphysical position is as remote as can be from those of Haavikko and Saarikoski. In our partially delusory relationship to the universe, seen askance, things are at once messages, spiritual correspondences, and masks symbolising and concealing the unavailable *Ding an Sich* – the 'it itself' of Haavikko. Where everything is an apparition, it is not surprising to encounter an apparition:

> An ancient man came to meet me on the riverbank,
> a cut thread in his wrist.
> The moon shone through him and through his entrails,
> his shade's heart pulsing like a lampwick.
> He laid his old hand on my head:
> The boat's waiting,
> no need for oars, or a wind.

Manner, as this vision of, say, Charon suggests, is a *vates* – implying a blend of prophet and poet: perhaps sybil or shaman is the appropriate word. A whole culture, a history of science, magic and perverted will are concentrated into a four-line poem, disguised as a sinister, absurd, agonised personal experiment:

> As a test, I set my will against the will of matter.
> Concentrated. Stared at a lamp. Battled all night long.
> Tortured the fragile threads. Finally the light flittered.
> Went out. Darkness came. I'd conquered.

This is a private occasion, but our love of darkness is not seen as an accident of history, but an evil at the root of the individual, contemplated with horror:

> Night's daughters are knitting shocking sights, quietly,
> red into black, black into red, uniting them.
> The anarchists' colours, aren't they, like death and truth?
> 666 – what's that? The number of the beast or rat poison,
> or a trio of six-winged angels?

I have made her criticism of the scientific post-Cartesian metaphysic appear more explicit than it is: mostly it is oblique, enigmatic, paradoxical, experienced on the senses and in the heart: 'I can feel the autumn light with my hand.' She creates a world of atmospheres, where everything is animated but evanescent; but the dreamlike state induced by the felt presence of death, whatever that is, and concretised by mist, is not dimmer but vivider than prosaic consciousness:

> Morning came to the meadow;
> horses were born out of mist.
> How quiet they were;
> one leant his head on his beloved's harness,
> his breathing rising warm, his moist eye
> gleaming in the daybreak.

His coat was like a kasbah carpet-weaver's
hand-woven pile,
his muzzle softer than a phallus.

Her cloak of mystery has not prevented her taking a keen interest in public and social interests in her other writings or made her lose her sense of humour, only lightly touched in here.

Eight of the twenty-one poets in this volume are women, chosen on their merits, not because they are women. Only two of them show feminist tendencies, Eira Stenberg and **Eila Meriluoto**. When I was living in Helsinki in the fifties two new names that seemed to stand out were Manner and Meriluoto. At that time Meriluoto had a Rilkean orientation and was writing sonorous melancholy meditations in triste metres. After great fame, she began to seem less prominent, but in the course of time a very edgy new note was coming into her work, which was also freer in metre and free of rhyme. Södergran's prophetic note had perhaps shaded her earlier work. Södergran's feminine protest now reached in her a new bitterness and even stridor. Moreover, the bitterness had spilled over onto the women themselves, onto their acquiescence in their exploitation:

We'd undressed ourselves ourselves:
all the half-finished tissues, all the soul's tangled wisps
yet again for the man, at his ass's feet.

As early as 1958 there had been a revolt against the very biological condition of womanhood:

So for this, was it, all that modelling –
the pelvis's fine and bashful curve,
and the roseate fragile line of the soul.
Not for the somewhere melodious
immaterial smile of a passing god.
No: for this: to form a gate
for the stranger – for the first stranger,
the ur-stranger, to enter in.
And for other strangers to go from, without a glance,
inconsequentially setting their courses
towards their particular fates and driving away.

In 1963 she announces:

No thanks, not for me,
any of that snug humdrum death,
mouse-faced fidelity round the pantry
(to cheese and the cat).

Yet clearly this is a woman for whom love has been not only important but sacred: 'I don't speak about this.' In *The Steps* (1961) she had written:

Some love affair: and nothing but a sea,
a tide of bloodspume surging through the limbs,
the body-hairs stirring like seaweed,
a stiff dry pain under the plenty, waterlogged:

under the boat today
(a midday shadow perhaps)
a black palm supporting us deep down,
ebony-wood gilded by waves,
looking quite beautiful from here.

Here passion is seen as pain, the basis and support of love and also something beautiful. Later it will emerge and be seen more clearly as pain: even then it will be beautiful, more beautiful. But pain it is:

As I wake in the morning, you're still in my life.
It's not the moment of truth
but of grief –
made from the same plush as love:
velvet, dark and difficult to maintain.

Stripping it off, I put on a pinafore
and clear up the end of the day alone.

Is this masochistic poetry? Well, it is certainly about the recognition, rejection and acceptance of suffering; and suffering is not always morbidly attracted.

Eira Stenberg is still more of a warrior. She's anything but a manufacturer of dreams. Is the knife she flourishes sadistic or surgical? Is it fierce maternal concern or unhealed wounds that make her recreate family love as a torture camp?

They're flickering blue flames,
those souls in the cots:
marsh lights in dim fens.
Only the heart can burn that way, smouldering on
without turning to ash.
The world reeks: the concentration camps
are set up at home.
Sooty: those slap-marks on the cheeks.
The barbed wire cuddles round us
and blooms with roses.

In 'Then He Came Back' (1979) it's the banalities of married life that get the stick. The poem, with all its fun and skill, is just a little too close to a complaint about who's going to do the washing up – but has a haunting ending:

It's bad luck to love a man!
He's a story without words,
sitting in his star and reading the paper...

Here I am in the kitchen!
The chores have suddenly gone childish

and started yelling for their mammy.
The table looks at me beseechingly,
whimpering to be wiped,
the pan's yowling – mouth wide open –
the floor's kicking, with its trousers down,
desperate for a cloth,
and the piano's baring its teeth like a cur
under its dusty fur cover –
God, this everlasting motherhood!

At dead of night the man comes home,
curls in my arm, grows small,
and the woman, slim of bones, broadens into a sea –
welcomes the ships groaning with hopes,
and turns into a harbour and forgets her name.

Her later poems (1983) have been more sinister, probing into the evil that comes out with the child at birth:

A child comes thrusting out of the firegrate,
laughing as it's born.
Only prophets laugh as they're born –
they know childhood's the worst betrayal.
She's decided to give it the slip.
Quick as a flash, she's milked her mother dry
and grown up. She can't cry.
For her everyone's heart is a fuse.
She runs out
into the street
and kicks to death
the first old lady.

Murder's going on in the home, even if undetected. There are enough hidings to 'make a birch-broom'. Lies drive the waggon, though for one child the horse is a Pegasus. All the latent and overt fury is not unconnected with the adult world outside:

The newspaper's obese
and half of it's horror
half flash.
It's a bloodstained packet of
pictures of Santa Claus.
Hold it carefully
or a stack of guns might clatter out onto the floor.

The politics of the family are the politics of the world, and vice versa. Stenberg seems to have come close to a secular rediscovery of original sin: a taint we are born with, nurtured and enriched by the family through example and extending to the conduct of the great world.

Sirkka Turkka is another strong persona, though she is not fighting anyone or anything, unless it is any negative thrust of destiny that might prevent her being herself or fulfilling her passions. She brings herself before the reader in all her fullness, passionate about dogs and horses, a passionate lover, a passionate mourner, thinking of herself and the horse Salome as 'two oddballs in an odd world', herself as 'the dud leading the dud'. Her sense of humour, the depth of her emotion, and her relish for phrase-making generate a very rich texture. In mourning, her keening is like the *agon* of a tragic heroine, but in reporting on the minor pains of being human she has a sharp eye for the absurd but completely expressive detail: 'The cock sleeps on the hatshelf in the hall.' In an interview she says 'There's nothing made up in my poetry', and for her life grows out of wounds.

The "pathetic fallacy" finds its way into her poetry as naturally as it would into a folk poet's, for it is part of her make-up to personify nature just as animistically:

> When I write of autumn as an old driver, I don't do it to embellish my poetry, but because that's exactly how it happens to be. I can't write poetry by consciously "making" it. It's truer to say that my poems write me.

I think we need to take that remark seriously when reading other poets in this volume. Whether that ancient animistic consciousness will be driven out of Finland by urbanism and technology is difficult to say, but it has not gone yet, and not from other minds too, who may not be writing poetry, or perhaps even reading it. Yet it would be a mistake to suppose that this cannot co-exist with sophistication. Turkka works at her poetry like any other professional:

> Another stage is the melting down and welding together of texts born at different times. It, too, is a fiery job, and I have to have a concrete physical contact with where everything comes from.

'Fiery job' reminds one of Blake, and there are many other things Blake would say yes to.

By contrast **Mirkka Rekola** believes that it is the words that matter, not their writer. 'Even as I speak I can hear myself keep silence.' She is an esoteric poet, not only in her personal reticence, but in the reticence of her poems:

> It's undeniable that poetry – read properly – can often be difficult, and that may be true of my own work...There are never more than a few people whose life is poetry.

Aphoristic in poetic style – as well as being a writer of aphorisms – she cherishes ambiguity of style as a mirror of the ambiguity of life. Her inner life is part of the universe too, but, paradoxically, that makes her different from other people who do not recognise this about themselves. Her poetry is a reminder. But in thus approaching others, she becomes alien.

As grass stone
life
touches me.

Like a haiku the poem asks us to consider what kind of 'touching' this is. What is the meaning of this contrast of sensitive and insensitive? – for she strikes the reader as acutely impressible. In what sense is she 'stone'? Is she speaking about being very close and yet inaccessible? Perhaps compassionate and detached, like a bodhisattva? The reader is being invited to be creative, and the poet is showing faith in the reader. As she says in *Autumn Changes the Birds* (*Syksy muuttaa linnut*, 1961):

Speech must be
as if my words
still had a voice
and you were saying it all in reply
to the one near you
in this wind
that comes from the beginning
and never stops winding over us and around us
here we are
so close in age
we could shout with a single voice.

In spite of an impression of distance, there is also an extreme impression of closeness; and moreover there are undoubted signs of passion and eroticism in these coolly sculpted poems.

The former Karelian refugee **Eila Kivikk'aho** is another poet of introverted reverie, glad to escape, like her fellow Finns, to a lonely lakeside. If there is the noise of a party in the house, she is likely to creep out onto the jetty and watch the changing pastel colours of those rather light nights:

Dew comes so quietly
and mist and morning.

Her poems remind the reader of what might be their own searches for meaning on the edge of the forest, as in 'Out of the Meadow' (1951):

Blue butterflies, a child's eyes
flitter after a buttercup.

But stairs ascend time
out of the meadow,
and eyes must light on other flowers:

the lines thought twists into
before it turns into fate.

Perhaps, for her, exile from her childhood Karelia is a kind of death-in-life, and her art death's recording of what life was. In 'Charcoal

Sketch' (from *Poems 1961-1975*), the burnt-out wood recalls the life of the tree:

The charcoal fills the paper
with a picture of its own burnt-out tree

leaves in their thousands
leaf-shadows

can't you see –
that's how green it was!

Satu Salminiitty, twenty-seven at the time of her latest work here, introduces a quite opposite, bold, life-relishing, death-accepting metaphysical *élan*. She trusts her intuition in its retort to materialism, and there is little irony or distress apparent in her work. Sensuality and passion are there in plenty, and a mystical faith:

Year by year
the mornings wipe the mind clean
till there's nothing there but a spacious head –
spaced-out as a convalescent's whose slowly-absorbing eyes

are meeting colours as if never before:
orange, green-aquamarine, pink!

Then too there's premature peace,
premature wisdom
for which punishment is in store.
The earth won't easily let go
its pets, its guinea pigs.

But no one's happier than I.
A woman: one hand's burning, the other's
protecting the flame.

Whether her optimistic critique of rationalism is a foretaste of something new, something peculiar to herself, or something passing even in her, remains to be seen. At this stage her books, uneven as they are, with their rocketing feelings, suggest the continuing power of renewal of Finnish verse.

Lassi Nummi's poetry, taking into itself a great deal of suffering, also seems the work of a temperedly happy human being, one tested by a lot of experience, but nurtured by sustained love, response to beauty, and the charm of art, which compensate for an equally strong sense of bewilderment, scepticism and a permanent sense of "leaving today". All these feelings co-exist with frustrated melancholy and dread, even cosmic horror. This openness is the openness of an essentially religious, slightly mystical temperament, susceptible to the dark night, highly intelligent, and philosophically inclined but sceptical of all formulations. A kind of cultivated faith retains a delicate balance on a world known to be volcanic:

Whom shall we tell it to –
this drive through the fog, across a moonscape
up to the volcano's booming and flames,
lava crackling, glowing and slowly, painfully
hardening into black stone.

Life begins with 'Thirst' (1956): a vast thirst for love that sobs with pain:

your sobbing in the night drinks an ocean dry;
my sobbing drinks an ocean.

At dawn we wander away from our shores.

And at noon we hug each other, with no tears on our lips,
on the ocean bed, in a desolation
with no shadow.

In the poems one watches these feelings maturing through 'love at second, third and even fourth sight':

The flagstones are white, lightly flecked and veined
like a woman's skin
who's not as young as she was
and someone still loves.

Till the poet looks at 'age's empty room', 'full of the coming winter's severe light' but also beyond to spring and 'a summer day's exalted stillness, where the curlew cries'. And (in *Double Exposure*, 1983):

In noon brightness
I turn and look.
In midnight blackness
I reach out my hand –
and touch.

Skin to skin:
the pass to being people,
woman and man.

There is always a thinking mind at work, but the poems are poems of listening: they notice evanescent moments and pick up sensations almost impossible to define:

Into sleep a voice:
churchbells.
I'm wakening to silence
to the solitary chirping of August's bird...

It is the moment of emergence from unconsciousness into semi-consciousness, when 'bluebacked appletree boughs are heliographing a raw barbarian eagerness for life' and an apple is 'concentratedly pondering its own ripening'.

Väinö Kirstinä shows the difficulty in reacting against a prevailing trend. As time passes the reaction seems less, the resemblance greater. 'Trying to break the mould of Finnish modernism – hermetics, for example', he brought in familiar details of other modernisms – fridges, trams, and so on. Yet his rhythms and much of his imagery are close to those of his contemporaries and even predecessors. In 1961 he was writing in *The Plain*:

> If you come to the windy country at the bottom of the sea
> the trees are few, the gales incessant
> from shore to shore.
>
> You'll get to see far
> without seeing a thing.

Presenting himself as an urban figure, in the country (as in this poem from *Life Without a Stand-in*) he has an almost Pan-like indigenousness:

> The quilt has slipped. I cough, swallow some cough mixture and water, smoke half a cigarette. Back to bed. It's spring. I keep clearing the riverbed of slush under the bridge, I'm helping the spring to come. Ice and mud accumulate under the bridge. The piers keep giving, the force of the current smashes the timber supports. Now I'm downstream. A surge is coming. I wade a mile or so downstream in frozen slush, opening the channel. A surge is coming behind me, but it hasn't got to me yet. I'm Kirstinä of the Spring.

Or, more comfortably:

> The rye outside my window is growing
> like a great stiff giant.
> I go to the window and look out:
> the weather's brightening up like a shattered ice-sheet,
> and the corn's growing with a crackling noise.
> Of all this I'm the father.
> I open myself to the floating caresses of the air.

Otherwise:

> I live in an industrial city
> sometimes we ring up in the night
> there aren't many of us here

Loneliness and *angst* in the city recur in **Pentti Saaritsa** too:

> In the bowels of each apartment block
> there's always that one unidentifiable sound.

With no metaphysical consolations, he seeks solace in the physical: 'Ear and armpit, they're a cosmos.' Or in music, so often invoked as imagery:

> From the former note to this one is a tritone:
> a far-away French horn against
> a tempestuous forest of strings.

His sensuous and haunted solitude exists, worrying, though often ecstatic, in a more than slightly threatening universe; he hears 'the throat-clearing death opens the dialogue with' yet again; but it is:

> a moment when life
> is longing to show itself so completely one
> you could cover it with a single poignant feeling
> and write the whole thing off at a stroke.

As the winter storms pass there is:

> a sky like a Greek sea
> and a sun that stains the city's fumes
> into favourable omens of good decisions.

Risto Ahti's slightly belligerent mysticism and distinctive prose rhythm give him a very custom-made look, but he has learned from his predecessors and contemporaries. His didactic eroticism and surrealistic non-stories are critical, aphoristic and visible signs of restless search. But they are celebrations too of life as part of a larger life, to which he seems to have access. Not trapped in a conscious or unconscious deterministic scientific metaphysic, he is moved by love or rage to challenging affirmations, appropriately dramatised:

> I admit it, I love many people, everyone, when I'm only loving you. As night meets day, nature goes quiet; even the wind goes mute at this frontier.
>
> How wildly and bewilderingly the morning light pierces you!
>
> It was always so quiet when we met. What I loved most was when the pressure in us pulled our mouths dumb. All at once, we were not being, yet being; nature roared around us, piles of stones turned into mountains, the flowers stretched to the clouds, the grass-tips touched the rooftops.

The title of this poem is 'Shame, as a Source of Energy'. What is he ashamed of? Has he been accused of loving other women? It is the type of love, at any rate, that seems destined ultimately for God. On the way, however, he loves a woman who lives 'as if life were pure wedding rites'. Her dress says 'Danger: poison'. Yet it is a risk he is willing to take, and as she takes it off her nakedness is the dress of a queen.

Nothing could be more of a contrast than **Jarkko Laine**. One of his greatest pleasures is sniping at various ecstasies, whether religious, poetic or erotic. Laine's dissatisfaction with the the inherited images of both poet and sage amounts to a passion, as in his poem 'The Poet. Is he the Mad Englishman Who Staggers to his Feet in the Music Hall and Bellows "Jingo"!':

> What is the poet's task?
> To be Hamlet cantering up and down cemeteries
> letting off portentous verses
> at mossy stones?
> To construct a guillotine in the sitting-room corner
> and stand there practising courtly bows?

Drink weak coffee, get metaphysical?
Press his face against the window until the winter glues him to it,
sneer at the passers-by,
exhibit his heart struggling like a snail to get out of the mud?

His satirical scorn sometimes bids fair to destroy his feelings: his hatred of humbug can seem stronger than his will to live. A critic all the time, observing himself as if he were a reader of himself, he is very conscious of his audience, and never short of something to say: his misanthropic talent is more urgent than his distrust of art. Nevertheless, he has so much relish in the work of demolition that he almost comes across as good-humoured.

Of the poets born in the fifties, **Arto Melleri** is the most flamboyant, drawing on his theatrical talent, and improvising bravura obbligatos on the decadence of culture;

Some day every pleasure dome turns into
an underground dungeon, dawn
casts on the French chalk
the shadow of a grill.

Germany still seems haunted by nightmares, Greece needs a shower to wash off some of the dust of its history, Zola is the first of the media writers, a walk across a marsh recalls Dunsinane, and 'The Wind is Whistling Through Europe's Windows':

I watch the darkened television:
one town after another
is rising up against its town plan, crumbling
to rubble, the refugee camp
is housing for our time.

In a broken-down house
a poor wife's celebrating:
now she's rich, Hollywood's splintered light
has turned the tinsel in her ears to platinum…

He is one of those writers who cannot become accustomed to the fact of Buchenwald and Hiroshima; but the passion this generates makes him write like a Jeremiah with some affirmative possibility in mind that mankind is ignoring.

Ilpo Tiihonen's experiments with loose rhyme and metre show that they can do new things, when coupled with street language, slang, new wrenched rhythms, and a gallery of down-and-out characters, as well as friends, relations and members of his own family. He is strongly opposed to the miniatures that appear elsewhere in this volume and uses comedy as a deflationary device. His poems can bring Brecht to mind, but a more sentimental Brecht. The drunks and city lights co-exist with a more-than-latent romanticism, and his irony can easily reveal its underbelly of tenderness and nostalgia. The more extravert gestures of Tiihonen and Melleri are in fact not too different in their ultimate inspiration from the introversion of some of their elders.

There is no doubt, though, that this younger generation either has more hope, or is looking for more hope, than that which came to maturity during or just after the war – understandably enough.

Pentti Holappa, of that older generation, is the only poet here to have had an official position in politics, but he, like the rather younger **Hannu Mäkelä**, who has had a very active life in publishing and created a prolific variety of prose, obviously considers that the field of poetry is the interior life and the awareness of one's cosmic situation. In both there is the same attentiveness to the minutiae of feeling and consciousness, as they play observantly round the detail of the current and passing moment. In this they are closer to the sensitivities of Kivikk'aho than the satirical, linguistic and socio-philosophical weight of Haavikko and Saarikoski.

I should now like to take a closer look at the latter two poets, who are generally considered to be the major voices of that older generation.

IV.

Haavikko's foreign literary stimulus came from Eliot, Saarikoski's from Pound, though not politically.

Paavo Haavikko was impressed by the translation of Eliot's major poems that appeared in 1949, when he was eighteen. He does not write like Eliot, however, and never did. What he must have found was not so much a model as a licence: to commit his own thinking and feeling to paper in their spontaneous order; not to fear obscurity; to be paradoxical; to enlist the creativity of the reader. He shares Eliot's illogical consequentiality, imaginative wit, use of surprise and inexplicit point of view. He juxtaposes contradictions, respects idiom, and resorts to a deflating humour and anticlimax, as Eliot does, in a perhaps not dissimilar "conservative" distrust of enthusiasm for change (unlike the political conservatives of today, eager, not to conserve, but to accelerate market mutability). In Haavikko's case dismay at the world has resulted in a perhaps paralysed semi-anarchist position. He has a feeling for the presentness of the past, though it is not necessarily a happy one, and he has no love of the traditions of the church: 'I don't wish to change this system. It's bad enough already.'

He does not attempt the symbolic sweep, musical structure,

cinematic montage, or dense learned allusiveness of Eliot. He writes plays, but his poems do not share Eliot's theatricality; there is some drama in them, but it is closet drama. His favourite form is the sequence: short, condensed, aphoristic, paradoxical, often humorous though melancholy organisations of abstract, contradictory pseudo-statements. The compression creates puzzles, but they are soluble:

> The fingers that make you a door are now
> occupied so abstractly.

Here a pregnant woman is counting on her fingers the months to birth: it is easy to see therefore that she is a door for her child, and that it was her love-making hands that made her so.

As well as a crossword-puzzling mind, the poems also demand a capacity, like Haavikko's, to deal in scepticism:

> I vote for spring, autumn gets in, winter forms the cabinet.
> Tell me whose lot you stand with, whose songs you sing
> with your mouth full of glass.
> I'm against socialism, capitalism, its, their crimes.
> I'm against their crimes, I swear, I share in them.

The poems may be set in non-existent environments, but they are like X-rays of environments that do exist. Fascism is when 'the state owns economic life, or, what amounts to the same, economic life owns the state'. This neatly eliminates the verbal distinction between the Soviet Union and the USA. It makes you think, though it may be a sleight of hand. Purifying the dialect of the tribe, the realist looks at actual behaviour, not the verbal smoke; then the poet creates smoke of his own to tease the reader into distrusting language. There is a rock, a certainty, under the shifting waters: distrust of power. Haavikko, in a wicked world, is not for socialism. 'The big moment is when the oppressed becomes the oppressor. That's when history takes a deep breath and starts lecturing.' Haavikko doesn't employ the lecture as a form, but his concisions, aphorisms and drama are lectures on power, the enemy of man that man cannot dispense with, as he cannot dispense with his irredeemable irrationality.

Power is a necessity, but it is ruthless, immoral and set on an uncheckable destructive course. What is impermissible for the individual is required for the organisation, whether it is the state, with its hired assassins and law-exempt secret machinery, or a business organisation, with its commitment to annual growth and elimination of competitors. 'I often entertain myself by translating historical events into the jargon of business management, or business promotion into war.' Or economic growth into biological growth:

The seedlings, the firs, need your help through the grass.
  For a year or two, perhaps five, they're grateful.
Then the grass needs your help to survive the trees.
  It goes bald round them,
                  around their majesty.
And the pine that grew fifteen years in an alder grove,
  three feet high, sinuous, bowed, bent with snow,
      starts to prosper.
It kills everything within reach
  for the next two hundred years, annually.
That's where it has to be.
  Never say it's growing in the wrong place,
      a tree.

This is a popular one-sided thesis: ruthless biological or cosmic liquidation, perhaps a model for man. But, one may ask, how has it allowed the planet, and vulnerable creatures like ourselves, to get this far? Are there no antithetical forces?

Perhaps Haavikko might think (though he does not say so) that this one-sided thesis can be medicinal, homoeopathic – itself an antithetical force? But I doubt it. There is pessimism and depression at the basis of Haavikko's work – which is of course no judgement of its validity: the work must be judged as work. Yet there is an appetite for life in his work, too, a *concern*, that is the reverse of pessimistic.

'Practise free will: rejoice at death.' This suggests that free will lies not in the choice of action or destiny, which is determined, but in a free choice of *attitude* to what you cannot avoid – not only death, but the events of life that are a chain of reactions. A deterministic view such as this is that of the recently prevailing scientific metaphysic, now somewhat modified, but its implications have never been fully worked out, certainly not translated into practical moral attitudes, or the legal system, which assumes that if you commit murder you do so freely, unless you are mad.

Like all disbelievers in free will – if he is truly a disbeliever (it may be an irony) – Haavikko is illogical and inconsistent: he behaves as though it exists, and as if his words and choices could be influential. Nor is he the anarchist, or practical anarchist, his distrust of power and pseudo-acceptance of cosmic self-aggrandisement might suggest. Implicitly, we are dependent for protection on the organised power that is destroying us piecemeal and will finally wipe us out. There are times when he seems to be proposing joy in acceptance of destruction: sardonically he advises that aid to developing countries should be speeded up – this will escalate arms development and thus bring closer the world's final catastrophe. This apocalypse he calls 'the time of eternal peace'. Even now it can be enjoyed in anticipation – the only peace we are likely to encounter: 'The children's cruel games last till evening.' 'This world is already lost. I contemplate it with joy. It no longer exists.'

I take such nihilism to be an irony – an imaginative and alarming one, a temptation not only to him, but to many others, though not to me – but it may not be an irony. Yet the poems implicitly and explicitly promote formality in personal life, art and government; and this must surely be prophylactic as well as aesthetic. He likes some of the ways things happen in nature – slowly, recurrently. He distrusts size – big plans, big countries, big organisations. Though we have no free will, perhaps the freedom we appear to have is preferable to projected hypothetical freedoms?

It is surely a concern for security, as well as irritation and frustration, that makes him promote wariness about language. Why should we distrust language? Language can 'usurp reality', make what can be said sound as if it *is*. This theme is probably the main one in the teasing games of *Winter Palace*. A syntactic arrangement can wrongly suggest wisdom, logic or truth, when it is only an arrangement of words or a copy of a pattern in our minds. Haavikko tries to train readers by setting verbal traps. Certain words shuffle their meanings or stare at you with their inherent vagueness, in a parody of political language, among the conflicting precisions. 'The people' – what does it mean? The voters, or their representatives? 'The world' – a recurrent vagueness: it can mean the cosmos or various notions of society, but what does it mean in Haavikko?

'There's no such thing as profit in the world. It's a concept and object of book-keeping.' Are ledgers not in the world? We know that profits are made and exert economic and political power. The sentence must disintegrate into its ambiguities before we can take its superficiality seriously. What is 'profit', as opposed to ledger-entries or consumer articles? The 'world' cannot be the business world. Is it the loving interaction of human beings, or the cosmos? Almost certainly neither, but the question has been provoked.

'On a high hill truth stands', and, as Donne added, he who would reach her 'about must and about must go'. Are we not also in the *presence* of another order of truth, which is permanently introducing itself to us, concealed perhaps by its magnitude, as well as its smallness, and by our mystification of ourselves and others, the connivance of language, the limitations of our perceptive apparatus. When we witness the phenomenon, are we also witnessing the noumenon, the *Ding an sich* itself?

> You can be certain that it itself,
>   not another,

no one else,
        has been introduced to you,
the world itself:
            it's not some allegorical creature
        celebrating ancient rites,
and that's why you couldn't quite catch its name,
        for it talks confusingly fast
and about everything at once.

It is a measure of Haavikko's irony – or perhaps of respectful indulgence to him – that it is possible to find this poem quoted as if it were a straight opinion and not a teaser; and at times one worries that it might be a straight opinion.

One doesn't need to be sophisticated in Kant – and Haavikko uses Kant in one of his titles – to see that what we can *not* be sure of is that the world is what it appears to be, if only because it is mediated though our own limited physical apparatus and subjectivity, itself shaped by language, and in a largely manufactured environment. 'The world' would look very different to an ant, an owl – or, indeed, another citizen. Yet, of course, it *is* there – 'it', 'itself' – but saying so much and so fast that we cannot take it in. And yet, again, 'the world' for late industrial man is almost entirely a human artefact – even nature is human-shaped – and therefore very much 'celebrating ancient rites'. The poem presents us with a cluster of problems disguised as solutions.

An uncritical reading of Haavikko would be worse than useless: dangerous:

The male seeks himself, woman, God, the tribe, age, the grave.
  A seeker, unappeasable by less.
Twins, half a person, a single fate, firm proof
  that a person is formed before his birth.

Here again we are confronted by a relentless determinism: man's 'fate' is formed 'before his birth'. But does Haavikko – who elsewhere writes 'And he who believes in scientific thought has irretrievably ceased to be a thinking human being' – accept the dubious 'evidence' from twin-studies as 'firm proof' of genetic determination? Does he believe in genes as 'fate'? Does pursuing Haavikko's list of generalities imply that all the individual's more specific pursuits are determined? Are the pursuits Haavikko lists merely consecutive – or are they summed up in 'the grave'? If so, is the pleasing variety of the multiverse sententiously equated with death, and is all pursuit thanatos? If we are to take Haavikko seriously we must often disbelieve what he says. Uneasily, at times, one thinks he means it. And if so, one would have to think less of him.

If individual fate and the general world are determined – therefore unreformable, by socialism, for example, or conservatism – why create political aphorisms? Because one cannot do anything else, like breathing? Surely a stage in determinism would be a realisation of determinism, whereupon one would realise the absurdity of one's actions, and simply stop? Are one's aphorisms not only determined but compulsive even after the realisation of their origin? Perhaps so?...

Well, one could go on at book-length, and Haavikko would have made one look ridiculous. Haavikko is challenging the liberal, yes, but chiefly he is attacking words; and anyone who accepted him too readily would make him look like a poor thinker.

Winter Palace is perhaps his most wonderful piece – a playful, and yet passionate, send-up not only of the whole poetic enterprise, and the poet's relation to the reader, but of the universe itself, and the futility of human generation and death. As he says:

> O straightforward word-order, from which
> there is only some occasional exception,
> all the crookedness of straightness,
> which is all-powerful!...
> I want to be silent about everything language is about...

But he is much more than a deconstructionist writing for deconstructionists: he is a man of subtle perceptions, evanescent awarenesses, moods, an observer of personal and communal tragedy, love and the politics of love. His quietly erotic, anguished, tender and sometimes cruel observations of women are not the least of his disturbing dramatisations. Yet it is obvious he has no consolations or solutions to offer, only problems and confusing clarifications: the unresolved problems and confusions of the intellectual and moral debacle of our century, presented bleakly, inventively, without hope, and as a challenge to the comfortable assumptions of those who accept the intellectual and political currency of our time without enquiry. Moreover he speaks from a position of strength and knowledge, not only as a survivor, but as one who has mastered the skills of our time.

His pursed smile, generous lips, neat now-greying head and beard, and shrewd, sad, thought-softened eyes, are as enigmatic as his books. Yet the enigma is not an unfamiliar one: it is the 'fate' of the intellectual who is unable to think his society out of its delusions and into integrated experience. He is the thinking representative, the consciousness, of unthinking modern man – and not of Finnish man, except as a starting point. He speaks for Europe, Asia and America.

There is nothing neat about **Pentti Saarikoski**. I remember him in a Helsinki bar in his early twenties, a confident young man with short black hair and a big grin, enjoying his fame, and drinking too much out of an apparently celebratory recklessness. He was changing everything:

> I read some cardboard cut-out poets
> with speech coming out of their mouths like writing;
> the poets were sitting on wooden stools
> in two forests and listening to the moon.

When I saw him twenty years later at one of the biennial Lahti 'Writers' Reunions', I was astounded by the alteration. Shaggy, unkempt, with a *Kalevala* beard out of Gallen-Kallela or Simberg, and a red dome of a decorated skull-cap that made him look like the priest of some Arctic cult, there was nevertheless mischief in his eye. He knew that as the physical incarnation of the mythical backwoods-Finn he represented a funny statement that he nevertheless took seriously as well.

No one found the disguise more ridiculous than this free spirit himself. He had looked like the young Lorca; now he looked like the ancient Väinömöinen of Finnish myth. As the translator of Homer and Joyce, he probably thought of himself as a Bloomian Odysseus and, just before his death, defined himself as 'a bad boy, forever running away from what he's longing for'. The insight explains why he was representative too: the articulator of a common 'fate', as himself, an existential wanderer, fooled and disillusioned by politics and his confused commitments. Thrown into a ruined post-war Finland, fired off from his essence and not yet arrived at his new essence, fending off both death and a threatening integration, yet realising that the Minotaur at the centre of the Labyrinth is perhaps a gate, to a possible way forward, he descends into darkness. Advancing unbeatably among the stones, getting perhaps a glimpse of the stars at the end, he reminds humanity of its modest humanity, and ends up with a Lear-like simplicity – or sentimentality?

> I'm not afraid of anyone. I love the world's people.
> I wish everyone well,
> my policy is
> we should love one another –
> not argufying but reasoning together like friends.
>
> Like bilberrying together.
> We'd heat up the sauna.
> We'd sit on the jetty after our dip,
> puffing and blowing.
> We'd behave.

As in the early poem fusing Dionysus and the senile urban alcoholic, no one is too contemptible to be rejected. There is acceptance of life on its often harsh terms. We are only partly responsible for ourselves, but the difficulty of creating a modicum of humane social reform is a conundrum. Saarikoski sets an example by displaying his weaknesses without shame; and his friendly concerns, if not always successfully skirting sentimentality, are an interesting contrast of tone to Haavikko's restatement of ancient stoicism in, for instance:

> The best of man is his short duration,
> that he disappears
> once and for all.
> Dead from the world's foundation
> till his birth,
> why should he wake up to do things
> that'll last for ever?

This may seem curt, but if you have no faith in religion and no faith in an earthly utopia, is it what remains? Ordinary human beings do not confront the implications of their own thought, whereas Haavikko heroically follows it through to its iron conclusion and surprisingly does not commit suicide and even seems to remain cheerful, active and competent. Is Saarikoski is a lesser man because he is weak and reaches around for love, consolation and hope?

Starting as an obsessed poet, half-ascetic, half-hedonist, faithfully attending his university courses on folk-poetry, Greek and Latin, but not graduating, Saarikoski moved effortlessly into print. Then he 'read Pound and became a Communist'. He must have seen in a modified ideogrammic structure a potentiality for welcoming a wider range of subject matter and response than earlier forms permitted – from the amorous and political to the satirical and comic, and perhaps the semi-mystical. Poundian rhythms, an over-eager response, not unmodified by irony, to Khrushchev's communism, a heady balance of conflicting ideas in equilibrium, made him bring his mercurialism, bounce, dash, political consciousness, social defamiliarisation and insouciance to a nation that needed a cheerful transfusion.

He transformed Finnish culture with his translations of *Ulysses, Tropic of Cancer* and *The Catcher in the Rye* alone. Inventing equivalent styles, he brought Helsinki argot into books for the first time in a radically transforming way. His own poetry remained, however, pure in language, idiomatic, slightly tongue-in-cheek naive without being *faux naive*. The poetry is in the rhythm, the subtle music, the observation, the juxtaposition, the implication. The occasional surrealistic note is controlled by rational implication and satire.

He has been uneven, though, in both thought and manner. After a kind of breakdown of time and causality in his late 1960s work, he resumed the search for a coherent and rational view, and his best work must be the very early and the late.

He early fell foul of the communist stonefaces, and as his hopes expired for anything he regarded as politically serious, a core of gaiety began to get overlaid with pessimistic and rather tired inflections. There were times when his work seemed to be sinking into a kind of boozy vapidity. Perhaps he had only imagined that socialism could be an ally: 'Socialism's yearning is different from mine.' The word translated as 'yearning' is close to the French *ennui*, crossing longing with boredom. The epigram, often quoted in Finland, loses its edge in English. In the original context I tried 'Socialism's dream is different from my dream'.

Or perhaps he had fallen for that foul infirmity of poets, thinking politics would be good for his poetry. But he was a serious, if frivolous, artist, who eschewed solemnity, and was obviously determined, in spite of all his conscious human limitations, to produce something that would not die. Increasingly he returned to the classics, Catullus, and the pre-Socratic philosophers, connecting them with his everyday banal or intimate experiences and the dear trivial items around him, as he picked blackberries and mushrooms, boiled the potatoes or observed the changes in the snow. Memories of historical tragedies, past and contemporary, memories of friends, worry about the world, worry about himself, adjustment to sickness and death synthesised.

The edge of satire never entirely went from his increasingly meditative and poignant verse. He sought to assimilate rather than remove his conflicts by watching them mirrored in the myths that suggest the permanence of these conflicts. A poet who had wanted to change the world, and did change people's awareness of it, he left it, conscious of being a very imperfect man, whose wisdom was a celebration of the painful acceptance of weakness. He found, as Auden did, that 'poetry makes nothing happen'; yet also that it survives, 'a way of happening, a mouth'.

Saarikoski's central images in his last trilogy are four: the labyrinth with the Minotaur at the centre, but no Theseus; the snake, the dance floor on the mountain, and the rowan tree. If we cannot directly influence the powerful political and economic organisation of our lives, or escape from the world's history or our flesh, we are free to modify life in the labyrinth with sometimes useful, sometimes useless but valuable little tasks, expeditions into the healing parts of our self and nature, and celebratory expressions of the life within us.

The Obscure Dances, his last book, partially translated here, and the third of the trilogy, is surely his masterpiece. In it he has found a loose but rhythmic form of both syntax and recurrent imagery that cures the sometimes prosaic structures of previous books. Even in *Invitation to the Dance*, the second book of the trilogy, many of the poems do not dance: interesting as they are, as narratives, or information on the human condition, they often deliberately emphasise their stumbling progress. The light and dancing organisation of the last book goes with some new spiritual music that Saarikoski appears to be hearing with the recurrent announcements of death.

The poem is a dance of a pseudo-Heraclitus. Heraclitus's nickname was 'The Obscure', and Saarikoski plays with the ambiguities of the name. Though he identifies with Heraclitus, the views of 'The Obscure' are Saarikoski's, often very different from what we know of Heraclitus's, if not opposed. It is Heraclitus's independent contemplation of reality that he identifies with, and through the name he reminds us that the hidden self of everyone is obscure, its obscurity becoming more apparent as it begins to return into obscurity.

There is perhaps a sixth of the book here, enough to suggest the recurrences and the variety. There is some delicious fun in the book, and some sly awarenesses of how the world works; but the poem undoubtedly gets an extra poignancy from the internal evidence of Saarikoski's consciousness of dying, and his slow experiencing of it, and of himself, warts and all, with love and humour.

The composer Nielsen said 'the death rattle is a phenomenon of life', and these poems are affirmative of life lived to the end. Underlying it all is Saarikoski's anguished experience of loss, perhaps of promise, certainly of friends, who still live with him as ghosts.

The potatoes have to be dug up and cooked, the mushrooms picked and casseroled, the blackberries collected. The poem begins with the announcement of his coming death, as the girl licks her ice cream and tells him 'I'm the light that leads you into darkness'. She makes intermittent reappearances, and The Obscure can only listen as she tells him 'don't found any clubs or corporations' or tells him he's daft: in the dark there are no colours. As he pushes his boat into the dark water, he does not know 'where the sea will take it or who will unload the freight'. At the end the girl comes again – he'd like to kill her as he is scared of death – but she tells him the Minotaur at the centre is now sleeping; and in that peace he can go with her 'to the dustbin' but also to see, if not colours, 'the stars again, the fragments of sky', both like and unlike Dante. She tells him there are a lot of blackberries he didn't pick.

Perhaps only this last volume is completely satisfactory as a whole. Yet all his work was its gestation; it is not only dignified by his death but dignifies it, and there were a lot of blackberries he did pick on the way. I find it significant that, as a Karelian exile, he wished to be buried in the cemetery of the Orthodox Valamo monastery on an island of Lake Laatokka, or Lake Ladoga.

V.

'Tradition', as Eliot pointed out, is not something we inherit like an estate. It is something we go out to, select and bring home. Dante, Laforgue and Donne were not part of the English *tradition* until the American poet made them so.

Selectively, and with a good digestion, Finnish literature assimilated Eliot, Pound, Henry Miller, Robbe-Grillet, Genet, Salinger, Swedish poetry of the forties, Japanese poetry, Södergran.

The Finns could not draw on their seventeenth- or eighteenth-century masters, for these were virtually non-existent. For six centuries, up to 1809, Finland formed a joint kingdom with Sweden. For much of that time Swedish was the language of government and official culture. To obtain an education you learned Swedish and Latin in a Swedish-language school – and you changed your name to a Swedish one.

Finnish began to revive, as part of a liberation movement, between 1809 and 1917, when Finland was a chafing Grand Duchy of Russia. Educated Finns were now changing their names back to Finnish ones and cultivating their often scant knowledge of the Finnish language, still very much alive, not only in the discourse of the peasants, but in their vigorous oral poetry. Finnish now became a tool of the privileged class, to liberate themselves from a Czar, who, though not the Czar of Finland but the Grand Duke, was increasingly felt like a Czar.

Elias Lönnrot, for instance (1802-84), became Swedish-speaking when he went to school at eight. As a young man he went round the villages, mostly in Russian Orthodox Karelia and Ingria, collecting the songs the peasants and serfs had never stopped singing since the Iron Age. He then Homerised the narrative ones into the national epic, the *Kalevala* (1835, and then a version nearly twice as long in 1849), and collected the lyrical ones into the *Kanteletar* (1840-41). Like Yeats in Ireland he was attempting to define the country's primeval identity in order to inspire present and future self-discovery.

Modern Finnish literature took its greatest impetus from three men: Lönnrot, with the *Kalevala*; J.L. Runeberg (1804-77), who, though writing in Swedish, imaginatively fused the Finnish milieu and folk poetry with contemporary European influences; and the economist and banker J.V. Snellman (1806-81). Snellman became a kind of impresario of Finnish literature, and the principles of patronage he established are still operative. Of course, the work was going forward in the other arts too – in the paintings of Akseli Gallen-Kallela, for instance (1865-1931), and the music of Jean Sibelius (1865-1957).

The *Kalevala*, about the struggles of two shamanistic peoples, Kalevala and Pohjola ('Northland'), for long defined the Finns' relationship to their landscape and climate. Haavikko still draws on it for narratives and scripts. Its tales dramatise the pursuit of power and woman: the old and young yearn, womanise, battle, sing each other literally into the ground; but they do so in a visionary landscape where love and death and the borderlands between this world and the otherworld have blurred boundaries. It's all done through story, and because shamanism was as ingrained in the storytellers as money is in us, the stories incarnate a shamanistic poetic psychology. Old Väinämöinen does not realise he's been driving Aino to her death and has to be warned by her spirit in the form of a fish that he had virtually tried to eat her. This particular story owes somewhat more than usual to Lönnrot himself, it seems, than to his sources, and yet it is thoroughly in the spirit of those sources. The stories mythologise but never forget the realities of fallible men and women and survival in the natural and political worlds. The climax is a destructive struggle for power: the Kalevala men fight Northland for the Sampo, the magic mill that grinds out wealth – namely corn, salt, gold and magic, everything a person needs. Broken in battle, it falls into the sea, but one fragment floats to the shores of Finland, securing eternal felicity for the country.

The *Kalevala* is now more accessible than it has ever been in Keith Bosley's new translation (OUP, The World's Classics, 1989). Bosley has been able to imitate the weaving repetitions, formulae, parallelisms, imagery, and content, and clearly has a poetic affinity for the life depicted; and his witty and informative introduction summarises succinctly what the intelligent general reader needs to know about the *Kalevala*.

Aleksis Kivi (1834-72) was neglected in his day, but his novel *Seven Brothers* – not yet adequately translated – and his plays and poems have had tremendous influence subsequently on the Finns' self-definition. Esko, in *The Cobblers on the Heath*, is still accepted as an archetype by self-mocking Finns: severe, choleric, given to imaginative flights after hard drinking.

Kivi portrays two enduring aspects of the Finn: his cultural aspiration, and his almost erotic, mystical relationship to Precambrian rock, lakes, spruce, pine, birch, juniper, sphagnum moss and Arctic berries – and the traditional ways of enduring the severe climate. The seven brothers come into conflict with the village through learning to read; they escape to the forest, clear land for cultivation, build a log house. But here, supporting themselves with hunting and fishing like their ancestors, they are never truly out of sight of civilisation; and at last they return to their parish and their neighbours, chastened, matured, to seek, not Nature, but society.

At the turn of the century, the outstanding poet was Eino Leino (1878-1926). Here symbolism and 'national neo-romanticism' as Leino called his movement produced a style that can be divined from Sibelius, Gallen-Kallela, and the architect Eliel Saarinen, whose Helsinki Railway Station was one of the first great modern buildings. Leino wrote ballads on national themes, revived the old metres of folk poetry and foreshadowed the conflicts of the new century. Yet, admired as he is, it is difficult to see any influence of his heroic manner on the chastened, painfully reconstructing Finland of 1945 and after. The influence is undoubtedly there, but rather as a latent moral inspiration for the will to survive and a memory of something handsome.

The Russian Revolution brought autonomy. Stalin arrived personally to present it. But almost immediately there was an outbreak of bitter civil war between the Finnish 'Reds' and the Finnish 'Whites'. The Whites, led by General Mannerheim, a Swedish-speaking former long-serving officer in the Czarist army, won. Later he led the Finns when they were attacked by the USSR at the beginning of World War II.

An economic transfiguration of Finland began after 1945 under the demand for war reparations Finland was not organised to provide. Finland raised the capital and set to work to provide the ships and machinery. Instead of being two-thirds an agricultural economy, she became two-thirds an industrial economy. With the reparations paid off, Finland needed to go on exporting. Now sixty per cent of Finland's exports are metals, engineering (including whole factories and pulp mills), textiles and chemicals.

This has of course transformed styles of life and styles of writing. The fighting backwoodsman, maintaining himself by forest skills and magic, still lies not very deep below the surface, but the surface is one of urban sophistication and adaptation to the changing modern world.

Even now, forest industry and agriculture are the staple of the country in gross value. Finland, with its 60,000 lakes, is a low-lying plateau eroded by ice. The forest covers 70 per cent of a country the size of the UK, with a population of less than five million. A third of the forest belongs to the state. About 300,000 forest farmers own the rest.

Yet most of the population now lives in the south, with half a million people in Helsinki alone. The Finn is increasingly an urban person, breeding new generations of technocrats and executives, experiencing increased life-expectancy, social mobility, deracination and all the usual consequences of accelerated change. His cities are carefully planned: they look increasingly streamlined and efficient, with a Scandinavian cleanliness and lucidity in the airports, roads, window displays, and lavish, imaginative theatres, concert halls and cultural centres. Finland's architects are encouraged, with apparently little parsimony, even with some extravagance. The styles – classical, Russian Empire, Art Nouveau, Saarinen, Aalto, Pietilä – are deliberately accommodated to each other and live harmoniously together as neighbours. With all this, an extraordinary number of Finns are likely to have a beloved log cabin they can visit at weekends; from this they will cross-country ski and take a sauna by the lake.

The Finns have jealously preserved their temperament and fed their passion for their own landscape and climate into their design and technology: the rugs, the glass, the textiles, the architectural styles, the music, the poetry all have traces of that lyrical presence of the glacier-razed plateau. Like every culture, the Finnish is threatened by the consumer internationalism of the twentieth century, yet the Finns are more determined than ever to remember who they are. Reading these poems, we witness a unique people's communion and dialogue with itself, preserving its spiritual life though its art as well as its economy.

Sometimes patronisingly regarded as provincial by nations whose mere size, power and influence are their claims to unprovinciality – while they systematically remain ignorant of the literatures, and even languages, of other countries – Finland has shown, through its capacity to digest foreign cultures and turn selected aspects to its own uses, that it is the reverse of provincial. There is much other threatened cultures could learn about both survival and sophistication from a nation determined to preserve, develop and pass on part of its best treasure.

Note

There is one final point I must make. There is none of Finland's flourishing contemporary Swedish-language literature in this volume. My Introduction has pointed to the long-standing influence of Sweden on Finland, and that inheritance has not ended. In an officially bilingual country, something like six per cent of the population still speaks Swedish as its first language – slightly different, chiefly in intonation, from mainland Swedish and called Finland-Swedish for convenience. Centred mainly in the Western coastal districts and Helsingfors (Helsinki) this group includes all trades – farmers, industrialists, intellectuals.

At school, Finns are taught both languages, which of course are utterly different.

The Finland-Swedes have a very lively literature, including some of Finland's finest poets: Bo Carpelan and Claes Andersson are only two of the contemporaries with growing international reputations. I translated some of these poets in my *Territorial Song* (London Magazine Editions, 1981) and would very much have liked to do so again. But since David McDuff was expertly working on a comprehensive volume devoted to the Swedish-speaking poets, and my own volume was going to be necessarily large already, it seemed sensible to produce a parallel rather than a competitive text. David McDuff's *Ice Around Our Lips: Finland-Swedish Poetry* (Bloodaxe Books, 1989) has provided ample selections from the ten most important poets – lyricists, mystics, modernists, dadaists and satirists – in the period between the *fin de siècle* and today. He has also translated the *Complete Poems* of Edith Södergran (Bloodaxe Books, 1984) and Tua Forsström's *Snow Leopard* (Bloodaxe Books, 1990). In these books the interested reader will find great imaginative stimulation and increased understanding of this whole fascinating cultural territory.

Finnish poems often have no titles. In this book a large gap is left between untitled poems to show that these are separate poems and not further sections of the same poem.

EEVA-LIISA MANNER

BORN 1921

TAMMI

Born in Helsinki, with both parents in publishing, and herself living a very secluded life – part of the year in Spain – **Eeva-Liisa Manner** is nevertheless centred on the industrial town of Tampere. And, though highly introspective, sensitive to the point of clairvoyance, and metaphysically inclined, she is also a socially concerned poet, alive to political currents at home and abroad.

She may pass out of her body and see it ticking there like a clock, but it is our world she is witnessing: our world seen as partially illusory, but without comforting illusions: the water table is rising, and the cellars are slopping; if grief smoked, the smoke would shroud the earth; there are cartridge puffs on the book's pages, but also on the actual fields of blood; "breaking" is necessary for beauty.

There is a quality of desolation in some of her work that implies an unhappiness about the status of man and his cult of death. Even by the fire she shivers: 'the cold's under the skin, it won't go.' We are one, but 'a mist of gross logic' is separating us, and we are surrounded by 'Dead Waters' – her most recent title – suggesting stagnation, though perhaps a pause before a change of tide? 'Night's daughters are knitting shocking sights, quietly.' Behind them is a perhaps supernatural evil.

The desolation in her work might suggest a longing for death: but although there is undoubtedly a morbid dimension to her feeling-life, something essential to her art, making her vision possible, death is perhaps something positive, something that 'life' deprives us of: 'Illumination: that poverty too is a skin I had to creep into, out of the light, to see how dark this light is.'

And with all this, there's a splendid sanity in her work, a kind of super-sanity that can only appear morbid through its superperception of a common morbidity. Her desolation is an outgrowth of her social concern, her aliveness to political currents, at home and in the world at large. Her poetry, drama and prose form an *oeuvre* that heals by listening and recovering.

She has discarded both of her first two books from her *Collected Poems*. Though she is very much her own woman, something in the climate of the fifties helped her to define her particular malaise and voice, though her first book had been published 12 years earlier, when she was 23. For comparison, I have started off this selection with a charming poem discarded from the canon, 'Rain'. The very different 'The City', from the same 50s volume, though not one of her best poems, shows her more characteristic imagery and style already established. The two poems are indicative of the eruption taking place in Finnish poetry.

Her very personal sense of humour is only slightly evident here, but she has done some amusing "imitations" of Eliot's *Practical Cats*. Her success as a dramatist includes a nine-year run at the flourishing Tampere theatre; and she has done some important translations – showing her leanings – of Hesse, Kafka, Mörike and Shakespeare.

A selection of her poems was translated by Ritva Poom and published as a chapbook, *Fog Horses*, by Cross-Cultural Communications, New York, 1986.

POETRY BOOKS: *Mustaa ja punaista* (Black and Red) 1944, *Kuin tuuli tai pilvi* (Like a Wind or a Cloud) 1949, *Tämä matka* (This Journey) 1956, *Orfiset laulut* (Orphic Songs) 1960, *Niin vaihtuivat vuoden ajat* (The Way the Seasons Changed) 1964, *Kirjoitettu kivi* (Inscribed Stone) 1966, *Jos suru savuaisi* (If Grief Smoked) 1968, *Fahrenheit 121* (Fahrenheit 121) 1968, *Paetkaa purret kevein purjein* (Flee, Boats, with Light Sails) 1971, *Kamala kissa* (Calamitous Cat) 1976, *Kuolleet vedet* (The Dead Waters) 1977, *Runoja 1956-1977* (Collected Poems 1956-1977) 1980, *Kauhukakara ja superkissa* (The Awful Child and the Supercat) 1982, *Kamala kissa ja Katinperän lorut* (Calamitous Cat and Moggibottom Rhymes) 1985, *Hevonen minun veljeni* (The Horse, My Brother) 1988.

from **THIS JOURNEY** / TÄMÄ MATKA (1956)

Rain

Rain opens the sleeper's ears
rain opens the shadows for the walker
rain opens your listening, the promenade inwards.

Rain opens slow lanterns and twilight musings
fragile glass shells, blown bells
still lanterns and their rainy songs
Dilp pilp dop.

Rain opens the eaves to laughter
the gutters to melody, allegro grace-notes
for a prelude of wind and shadow
for a windy shadow's aerial passing.

Rain swings your brolly open like a wing or skirt
rediscovers a forgotten beat, a paper boat
a great jellyfish's sail, those eager ships.

The City

How the houses have spread,
how the gulfs have deepened, the water blackened
in this city, the streets'll soon be flooding,
the railings are rusted through,
the groundwater's rising, the cellars are slopping,
fear's rising, screened though
behind a strangling discretion,
behind flagrant crime.

Boats'll be needed soon – hear the roaring?
Take to the boats, forget your hats –
or plunge in bravely
and take the word past the distress lights.

from **THE WAY THE SEASONS CHANGED** / NIIN VAIHTUIVAT VUODEN AJAT (1964)

My room, with its forest fragrance,
reddens earlier and earlier
as sun sets;
the heart of the redwood is darkening,
the diffracted light is cold.
Evening is red and old
as an iron spectrum.

If grief smoked,
earth would be shrouded in smoke.
Yet this grief too has fire beneath,
my heart burns but doesn't burn out.

Footsteps pad on the stair outside the flat.
Footsteps come, go.
They're not the ones I'm yearning for.

from **FAHRENHEIT 121** / FAHRENHEIT 121 (1968)

Morning came to the meadow;
horses were born out of mist.
How quiet they were;
one leant his head on his beloved's harness,
his breathing rising warm, his moist eye
gleaming in the daybreak.

His coat was like a kasbah carpet-weaver's
hand-woven pile,
his muzzle softer than a phallus.

Was it real, or heart's hallucination, that
cold light?
Was I here, or where, or dead, or someone else?
The sun pierced the lattice-slats
and again I saw that child, slit by the slats,
but now her shadow was flaked – with snow.

And now put ice in your music.
It'll turn to mathematics.
Put ice in your music now.

from **IF GRIEF SMOKED** / JOS SURU SAVUAISI (1968)

When I read, some other thinks for me.
When I write, my hand thinks for me.
When I sleep I don't ask, Do I exist?
I exist and know I'm not free:
I can't deceive myself: I'm in a dream.

I open it by lamplight –
a yellowing book smelling of grass and mould.

I leaf the pages, and a sound like rain
ensues, and a light breeze passes

from page to page and across a battlefield.
Cartridge-smoke scatters like dandelion clocks.

Uproar. Silence. Many steeds are straying about,
and men without steeds. Through lattice slats

peasant sounds and smells. Swallows' shrieks.
Aniseed and cow parsley. Poppy, dandelion clocks

and the book's pages dotted with cartridge puffs.
The circle of soft lamplight invests a field of blood.

Though why should I blame a book?
I've no other way, have I,
to put my left hand in my right glove?

If the art of writing hadn't been invented,
I'd be inventing it now

The trees are bare.
Autumn
leads its ponies of mist to the stream.

Far far away the dogs are barking and barking.
Little carts come through a narrow gate,
one by one, driverless, and disappear.

That's how a ghost drives, they say,
if the heart sleeps beneath a holly.
But ghosts are only memories.

Night's coming early.
Soon it'll be a winter
like a well, deep and cold.

I don't know the being of things, their qualities I do.
I know your being, your qualities I don't.

How come this endless intrigue and caprice?
Coldness said scorchingly, scorching things coldly?

Square the circle – what a multitude of sides –
and begin again from the beginning: write on mist.

See what the writing hand does in the mirror:
everything the wrong way round.

from **FLEE, BOATS, WITH LIGHT SAILS /**
PAETKAA PURRET KEVEIN PURJEIN (1971)

Possession According to Ogai Mori

Three things are necessary to aesthetic experience
(said Thomas): clarity, harmony, and beauty.

And breaking, I add;
for beauty in itself is no longer beautiful –

and never has been. Hunters
know it: those who love

the creature killed for pleasure: that instant
of the life breaking in the eyes.

If it's true that when I go
I don't need to go alone,
that you'll come with me, riding the other horse,
the one whose coat shines earth-brown in the moonlight,
(itself half-earth, half-wind)

if it's true, your promise, if
you'll ride to the gate – it's hazy
(the grass is erect, the gale's dropped)

I want to go now.
I want you now.

Day's always failing here, snow always dawning,
even in summer. Earth's heart won't thaw.
And the ignorant lake observes like an iron eye.

from **THE DEAD WATERS** / KUOLLEET VEDET (1977)

One day I passed out of my body
    and looked at the clock in the next room.
It was ticking like a pacemaker.
My body was breathing still back there, my heart still beating
like a clock wound to tick for a fixed time.

I slipped back in my body and pondered the phenomenon.
This heart's flagging too, all clocks do,
throbbing still in my wrist,
knocking the ribs of my ship-shaped coffin.

I want out, another voyage, other craft
whose curved ribs I haven't carved myself
in this bowl of blood.

As a test, I set my will against the will of matter.
Concentrated. Stared at a lamp. Battled all night long.
Tortured the fragile threads. Finally the light flittered.
It went out. Darkness came. I'd conquered.

An ancient man came to meet me on the riverbank,
a cut thread in his wrist.
The moon shone through him and through his entrails,
his shade's heart pulsing like a lampwick.
He laid his old hand on my head:
The boat's waiting,
no need for oars, or a wind.

A weird grieving in the forest –
while the hamlet's sleeping.
A weird fragile grieving
like a child's weeping.
You open the door. You listen. Silence.
You close the door. There again.
Who's lost their way in the dark?
Who's been exposed to die?
Who's being drowned somewhere?
A long weird grieving
like a memory weeping, or a shade, or an echo –
right along the lake.

The lake's charged with causeless light.
Now one could pass far beyond evening,
fading out, like a photo
left in the sun.

A light and easy exit:
the fragile images exposed from light and matter
dim out, thin out,
pass back into the light.

Empty paths. Footfalls:
a bird scampering on the roof.
In the morning, mist
thick enough to spin wool from,
as trees spin their filaments
on invisible spindles.

A jetty, and two steps down:
space is white.
Across what void?
Or not a drop at all?
Merely a lost lake,
and a swan's wake on the water?

A distant hidden room
a harness-leather smell
a darkish coachhouse
a huge delay

And through a tight wicket gate
slipped childhood
and a pony trap came for us
rattling on the gravel

White gloves on the coachman
the flourish of a whip, a cracking lash

We drove through dappled groves
Light, grief, light,
memory, snow

And suddenly the coachman was gone
and mere hands held the horses
and were leading me I don't know where

Moonrise at midnight
searches earth like a cave.
A crime has occurred,
there's a knife on the doorsill.

A red moonrise
searches all the wells.
A crime has occurred,
there's blood in the well.

The moon wanes to dark.
Nothing has occurred.
Night, merely, and a tarn's eye
and wolflight and a footfall

and on the doorsill a fish,
and a slashed oak,
stone of the blood and a covered well,
and hypnosis of iron.

A mallard honks
and the grass is rimy with early-morning hoar.
Glasslike: a filmy tinkle.
A vertigo of yearning.
Late autumn. I shiver even in the fire's blaze.
The cold's under my skin, it won't go.

I thought it was a letter, thrown on the porch,
but it was only a gleam of moon.
I picked up the glow from the floor.
How light it was, the moon's letter,
and everything was sagging, like iron, over there.

Marie Thérèse Parodies: 18

(for Professor Anton Mesmer)

When I was blind, I could walk and finger the keys.
Anton cured me, and now I cannot.
I sidle along the wall, my hands are willing
  but the keys refuse.
And I'm terrified of light.
A candleflame struck me like a lightning-stroke,
science's sword, whitest and darkest of all.

I was baffled to see the Danube trees in the distance
and not reach and touch them.
Perspective I'd not yet discovered –
illusion among the illusions –
and my eyes were medieval, their camera naive.

Dear learned professors,
don't wake love, it's needless and cruel.
Don't heal the blind
if sight strips us of this nearer talent –
our keener audition of the night.
An image is mere reflection,
darkness is meditation's deeper blind.

Notte, Serene Ombre

We were coming down the Spanish Steps, and I
was babbling on about a lutanist-bird –
and it baffled your brains! Any harlequin
would have understood.

And suddenly: in the north – and the evening's
not riffling an album of leaves, for here there are no trees.
Wings riffle the air, and oars the water, that's rotting.
Pigeons strut cockily –
lute under wing – do you see?
Seedy pigeons: mere music and lice.

Night: a bright shadow, the swing of the wind,
that's all.
For though we're intimately together
in an infinity the hours circle
like skew Roman numerals on a steeple clock,
we're divided by a deep sleep,
a mist of gross logic, a wool of distant meadows,

with dead waters all around.

Nada

'No se puede vivir sin amar.'
'Si, se puede,' I said
and dressed myself in black
for the last masked ball.

And my mouth was full of dust
as if I'd wept my throat dry
(though I've not wept for fifty years).

Compañeros, I don't want your heavens –
the low lights, the false friends,
the streets of kisses,
the lies of flying mirrors.

I want to break the last seal,
the moon that gives no light,
the night where nothing shines.

EILA KIVIKK'AHO

BORN 1921

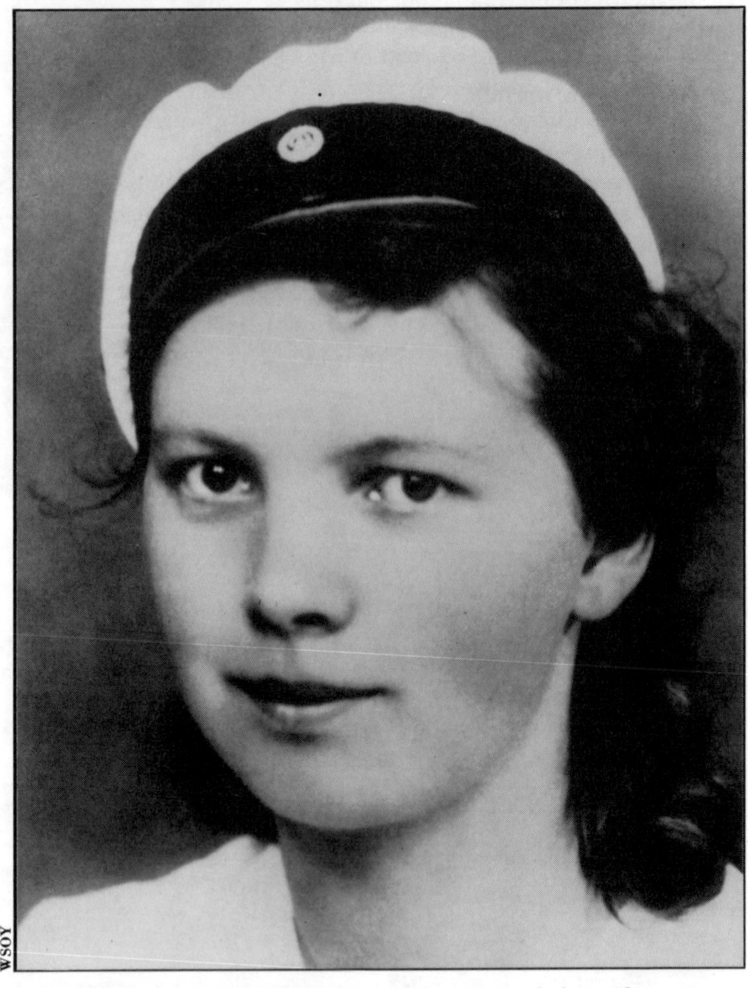

WSOY

The daughter of a shoemaker and uprooted from her native Karelia through its Russian occupation in the war, **Eila Kivikk'aho** has not lost an accompanying sense of spiritual exile. As a free-lance centred on Helsinki, she seems a wounded spirit in a world made without her, only rediscovering connectedness through art and solitude.

Her poems hover between the traditional and the modernist and cultivate an economical musicality. They make a cult of introverted solitude, but her relish of loneliness, her need to escape society, her intense response to forest and lake, appeal to a similar persistent need in many Finns and find a ready echo.

The neat, traditionally metrical encapsulations of emotion in her early work gave way to the new style in 1951, when she was thirty, with her third book, *Out of the Meadow*. Increasingly she has concentrated on oriental-type minimal statements, juxtaposing images and brief abstractions in musically organised insights and cherishings of the neglected.

She worked as a clerk until her mid-twenties but since then has lived as a freelance writer and translator, specialising in children's literature from English, German and Swedish.

POETRY BOOKS: *Sinikallio* (Blue Rock) 1942, *Viuhkalaulu* (Fansong) 1945, *Niityltä pois* (Out of the Meadow) 1951, *Venelaulu* (Barcarolle) 1952, *Valikoima runoja* (Selected Poems) 1958, *Parvi* (Flock) 1961, *Kootut runot* (Collected Poems) 1975.

from **BLUE ROCK** / SINIKALLIO (1942)

Drear Day

It's one of those days
when everything's too small, and
a paltry surge circles round
a diminutive tongue of land.

By pollarded willows
floats a boat of birchbark.
Under dwarf birches
I'm earthbound and dark,

all the grains of experience
weighing like lead.
Longing might be great,
but it too, it too is dead.

from **OUT OF THE MEADOW** / NIITYLTÄ POIS (1951)

Woman

If I were a tree
I'd tear myself up by the roots
under your window.

I'm a woman.
I wait for you
under the window.

Short Cry

Do you spend nothing but beauty?
Do you dig your home in a treasure
like rust
and eat it through?

Out of the Meadow

Blue butterflies, the child's eyes
settle on lovely buttercups.

But annual steps lead up
out of the meadow
and eyes must settle for other flowers,
the fatelines thought forms
before it turns to fate.

I'd Like

1

I'd like to sit on the jetty
alone with the lake
in its darkening,
as the wind quietens
and the mist rises.
I'd like to sit on the jetty
while the house shines with laughter.

Rise mist, cloak the house,
its bold voices, its lamplight.
I'd like to sit on the jetty
till the night's quiet.

2

Allow me a soft footstep,
the night I look at,
the night I'm in.

Dew creeps so softly
and mist and morning.

Only one soft footstep!
Hiding it, I slip away

from life into death.
Not to the past, not to the future,
not even from me into you.

Recollection

Words couldn't move mountains,
words weren't even up to opening my door.

But when you'd gone,
I took them in, to shelter in the warmth,
like swooned birds that had hit the window.

And they never tire of singing.
And I keep on listening to them.

from **BARCAROLE** / VENELAULU (1952)

Concealing the Innermost

Like a stiffened-to-a-twig stick insect
I want to be like
something no one
seeks for, looks at or stalks.

from **FLOCK** / PARVI (1961)

Flock

Migrating birds have their wedge
when they leave,
when the journey starts.

Once there,
it scatters, the flock.

A Lot of Talk

I hush up what I say with a lot of talk,
but the hemlock-pauses speak
and the cowbane, and the thorn-apples.

What I don't say
is the deadliest nightshade
that can grow on any house-corner.

from **POEMS 1961-1975** / RUNOJA 1961-1975 (1975)

Providence

Territorial song's opposite:
I grasped it:
no place anywhere.

Charcoal Sketch

The charcoal covers the sheet
with its own burnt wood:

leaves in their thousands,
shadows of leaf –

see how green I was!

KIRSI KUNNAS

BORN 1924

WSOY

Born in Helsinki, and the daughter of two painters, **Kirsi Kunnas** began as a writer of poetry for adults but made a great reputation with her revolutionary children's and nonsense verse.

Her poems are affluent in content behind their thrifty and playful exterior, translating into animal parables her imaginative and affectionate insights into real people.

The workaholic and hypochondriacal rat; the two snakes so in love they're gobbling each other up; the darling pussy fantasising crunching mice; the elephant whose thirsty trunk is making the rose cry; the crane for whom it would be 'a pain' if he looked like a crane: this wisdom, often erotically nuanced and taking the masks off recognisable neuroses, could be upsetting if it were not so disarmingly dressed up. But nothing is ever underlined, all is tricked out in a would-be innocent *faux naiveté*.

She continues to write accomplished, intensely musical and sensitive adult poems, suggesting a highly ethereal, mystical side to her nature – something one might not guess from her practicality and the playful irony and humour of her incisive children's poems. The richness of life is seen within a framework of space and light and ageing.

Some of the children's verses, which have played a big part in growing up in Finland, have been set to jazz on LP.

She has worked for a publishing house, is a freelance journalist, a writer of children's fiction and a translator, living in Tampere. She was chairman of P.E.N. for five years.

POETRY BOOKS: *Villiomenapuu* (Crabapple Tree) 1947, *Uivat saaret* (Swimming Islands) 1950, *Tuuli nousee* (The Wind's Rising) 1953, *Tiitiäisen satupuu* (The Tumpkin's Wonder Tree) 1956, *Vaeltanut* (Wandered) 1956, *Valikoima runoja* (Selected Poems) 1958, *Kuun kuva meissä* (The Moon's Image In Us) 1980, *Kaunis hallayö* (Beautiful Frosty Night) 1984, *Sirkusjuttuja* (Circus Tales) 1985, *Valoa kaikki kätketty* (Everything Hidden in Light) 1986.

from **BEAUTIFUL FROSTY NIGHT /** KAUNIS HALLAYÖ (1984)

Autumn –
  a toppled elk
    down on its side along the opposite shore
      loins shredded and eaten by rain and wind

will some night now
  scramble up the steps
    push into the house
      winded and snuffling

and muzzle out its smell –
  the familiar smoke of mutability
    in the cold house chimneys.

A wind sleeping in the raspberries
woke
  and whining like a hedgehog
    winding like a snake
      squirmed suddenly off.
        Guarding
what berries of Paradise?
      My heart's still
like a looting bird, panicked.

Dark, swallowing the sun –
a cuckoo forging the name of its egg.

Quick from the shadow stirs the mother bird,
with no bequest of her nest

but surreptitiously as if she
and her egg were still the same
spreads her legs on her changeling egg. Who

when you crack the shell, who
are you
  when you crack the shell?

Such insubstantial stuff:
the stars soar through me –

so chiffon-gauzy
I'm gone in myself and from myself –
a space of shining calm
a carolling cage and its freed
bird that does not fly.

from **THE TUMPKIN'S WONDER TREE /**
TIITIÄISEN SATUPUU (1956)

This Afternoon

It's just the sort of afternoon
when ants take off and land on the moon
and conjure with such powerful spells
that – open your mouth – it'll rain caramels.

Pussikins

Rosebud mouth and silky fur:
Pussikins, well, look at her,
sitting as proper pussies ought,
far away in thought.

Thinks Pussikins: oh what a treat
if there might be
a Mouse Tree, like an apple tree,
with dangling baby mice to eat.

When it was tea, I'd give it a tap,
and down they'd plop for me to snap.

Then she'd munch each juicy mouse,
warm inside her teatime house,
Pussikins, she would,
rosy little bud.

Crane

There once was a crane
   whose life was led
   as a uniped.
   He dangled his head
   and from time to time said:
      Oh what a pain,
      if I looked like a crane!

Woodpecker Song

A woodpecker's pecking, pecking and picking,
looking, looking for a woodpecker chick:
peck, peck,
          knocking and cracking
beaking and hacking,
pecking and picking at every nick,
ticking away like a lunatic!
             Chick, chick, woodpecker chick,
skedaddle home, and double quick!

Snakestrick

A snake met another
perhaps twin brother
and shuddered
as licking and flicking
it lovingly swallowed
its seeming brother,
while the other,
equally loving
and fit to burst,
pulping and gulping,
gobbled the first.

And each in the other's
tummy turns,
swallowing his brother
eternally squirming
and going all of a shudder.

The Pan and the Potatoes

Phew!

I'm sweating and steaming
I feel like screaming
I'm bubbling and seething
I'm rattling like tea-things
the pan said –
took his hat off his head – and
Phew!

I'm absolutely boiling
I'm bristling and whistling
and hustling and moiling
and all hot and sizzling
it's a mad mad bustle
the pan said –
took its hat off its head – and
Phew!

Ouch this hoppity, hoppity, hoppity
shouted the potatoes, popping up fit to split
no way of stopping it, dropping it, swapping it
dancing a polka, have to, dance, dancing a polka
got to go higher now, shoes are on fire now
galloping, galloping, off at a lollop
jumping and jumping and off at a wallop
turning and thumping, thumping and turning
oh this knocking and bumping and socking
off again copping it, hopping it, whopping it
makes me spit –
no way of stopping it

The Old Water Rat

There's a quiver in the reeds,
and a rustle through the grass.
Slop-slopping through the mud,
who's that puffing past?

Who's peeping there?

A whiskery jaw
and a muddy paw.
It's old Mattie
Water Rattie.

Squeezing water from his eyes,
a dewdrop on his runny nose,
he freezes and sneezes:
A-snee, a-snee, a-snizzery.
Oh what Misery!

Snizzery: sneezing misery –
it's trouble with sneezes.
Too many sneezes always displeases.
Snizzery's the water-rat word
for the thing that's occurred:
the need for a hanky.
A-snee, a-snee, a-snizzery,
Oh what Misery!

Old Mattie Water Rattie
is a workaholic
and a slave to duty.
Duty's beauty
for this sensitive dedicated Water Rattie.
Is he batty to get so wet?
It means he'll get
coughs and colds and nasty wheezes
and sniffly noses and beastly sneezes.
Well, it's how he's made –
to suffer for his trade.

But look, poor Mattie's taking a rest.
His cure is to lie with his feet north-west.
When his nose is due south-east,
that's when he seems to sniffle the least.

It seems to soothe and heal poor Mattie.

The Elephant Without a Name

Once there was an elephant
who with his hosepipe nose,
though nameless and inelegant,
sucked nectar from a rose.

He wished to ease his appetite,
although he could clearly see
that a rose is a rose and a rose's heart
is intended for a bee.

The rose's blossoms chose to be snide:
'Just look at Trumpetrunk!'
'Well, what I am I am,' he cried,
and, trunk in blossom sunk,

he sucked till he was drunk.
The rose soon started crying.
Soon he was crying too,
plucking prickles from his kazoo.

So he went
a long way
a long way away
a long

And he'll never never return
though he often dreams of the rose
and secretly sniffs her, to yearn,
whispering through his nose:

'Trumpetrunk! – my sensitive part!
How bitter these tears are to me!
But a rose is a rose, and a rose's heart
is intended for a bee.'

AILA MERILUOTO

BORN 1924

WSOY.

With her first book, at 22, **Aila Meriluoto** caught the post-war imagination of Finland. *Stained Glass* went through eight editions, 25,000 copies, in 1946-48. The sales are now 30,000 in this country of fewer than five million people.

Yet there was nothing sensational or meretricious about the book. These were musical, introspective poems, with a melancholy exaltation, influenced by Rilke and Finnish folk poetry, but distinctly individual and accomplished. Her translations of, for instance, Rilke's *Duino Elegies* and Martinson's *Aniara* show her interests.

The passionate disclosures in her diary of 1944-47 brought her new fame when it was published in 1986. The record evoked the austere post-war period in which, somewhat threatened by her growing fame, she was courted by older literary men, undergoing a sexual crisis, and discovering her own aware personality. The diary showed the sharp cutting edge to one side of her personality, which, at that time, was somewhat muffled in her dreamy poetry.

A difficult marriage to a powerful and disturbed poet, Lauri Viita, and living from 1962 to 1974 in Sweden hampered her continuing prominence before the public in Finland, though her poetry was developing in interesting new ways: loosening in form, becoming more explicit about the difficulties of love, the problems of being a woman, and ageing. Her poems were getting harsher without entirely losing their sensitive hypnotic feeling for symbolic correspondences. Her most recent volume shows that she still has that capacity for music and fantasy, which illuminate rather than turn away from the actual and the mundane.

POETRY BOOKS: *Lasimaalaus* (Stained Glass) 1946, *Sairas tyttö tanssii* (A Sick Girl Dancing) 1952, *Pahat unet* (Bad Dreams) 1958, *Valikoima runoja* (Selected Poems) 1958, *Portaat* (The Steps) 1961, *Asumattomiin* (Into the Wilderness) 1963, *Tuoddaris* (Tuoddaris) 1965, *Silmämitta* (Rule of Thumb) 1969, *Elämästä* (On Life) 1972, *Kootut runot* (Collected Poems) 1976, *Varokaa putoilevia enkeleitä* (Beware of Falling Angels) 1977, *Talvikaupunki* (City in Winter) 1980, *Ruusujen sota* (War of the Roses) 1988.

from **STAINED GLASS** / LASIMAALAUS (1946)

Grief's Spring

Grief's still in the bud. Like spring
it's waiting, with shut buds.
And look: these hands are buds –
these fists, clenched with dreading, hating –
grief's ripening there and waiting.

When their time comes they'll soften –
they'll open. They'll bloom into birth.
They'll be as long and shimmering
and lowly and silent as earth.
How lavish, you'll see – grief's spring.

from **A SICK GIRL DANCING** / SAIRAS TYTTÖ TANSSII (1952)

I've gone into my silence
and I'm going silenter still.
The summers flash across my land
and winters cover the hill.
And only when it's ripened
does the tree release its fruit.
So small is what I'm saying,
what's happening so great.

I'm big inside with a glitter –
the forests glitter, the fell.
But as soon as I extinguish
this land'll extinguish as well.
They don't understand, the others,
what I've been able to see;
they're deaf, and I'm a mute now,
and that's good enough for me.

Oh, I've gone into my silence,
and I'm going silenter still.
I'm big inside with my secret.
I'm silent and I smile.

Notburga

Day-long there'd been just one
decree in her: to work.
And with her sturdy, stooping arms
she'd bent, as a tree's branches
bend with deep arcs all day
to a driving gale.

But as the day wore on
the labour dropped like a wind,
and she stretched up straight, a young tree,
nightwards; standing there
with deep-hushed branches,

only distantly watching
the master yelling and yelling to go on;
and gradually raising her hand
she let the sickle go.
And look: it hung there in the air,
lifeless; proving that one thing is,
stillness.

from **BAD DREAMS** / PAHAT UNET (1958)

Burner of Villages

Behind us there's nothing, nothing at all.
Remember: behind us there's nothing.
There's only now,
the now of the footstep, recurring, recurring;
on our hot faces
the wind's cool now.
Now ends in eyes,
outside the village now ends in eyes
I can't see for darkness.

It's dawning.
Remember: behind us there's nothing.
Remember: now is nothing.
The time ahead is in two eyes,
it's all in two eyes I already see,
they're coming to meet me, in them
the whole burning village
is coming to meet me.

This

Under my hand
a sea of breathing swells:
a warm restful land.
Down winds the blood
and high: these ramifying veins
are full of the huge wind's sigh.

I listen, I admit: it is.

I don't speak about this.

Maternità

So for this, was it, all that modelling –
the pelvis's fine and bashful curve,
and the roseate fragile line of the soul.
Not for the somewhere melodious
immaterial smile of a passing god.
No: for this: to form a gate
for the stranger – for the first stranger,
the ur-stranger, to enter in.
And for other strangers to go from, without a glance,
inconsequentially setting their courses
towards their particular fates and driving away.

Expediency, ah! ah flesh!
Not untouchable, slowly mouldering.
Ah, soul that can be touched, oh soul,
continually rending a new soul from yourself,
and recovering, only to rend yourself again.
Scarred soul, in which even love
is a product, inescapable, purpose-designed.

Life uses you. Just like that, unceremoniously,
with a sneer at best, whisking you away.
And if some corner remains untouched,
the cloth's no longer useful. A corner of the soul, yes.
Not tragic. Merely useless in future.

from **THE STEPS** / PORTAAT (1961)

Love

Earth lurks into shadow like some beast
and the waters reach for the moon.
Your maleness reaches for me
and a milky wave of moonlight
throbs forward along the path.
In mid-shadow lies tomorrow
with all its divisions.

New

Some love affair: and nothing but a sea,
a tide of bloodspume surging through the limbs,
the body-hairs stirring like seaweed,
a stiff dry pain under the plenty, waterlogged:

under the boat today
(a midday shadow perhaps)
a black palm supporting us deep down,
ebony-wood gilded by waves,
looking quite beautiful from here.

from **INTO THE WILDERNESS** / ASUMATTOMIIN (1963)

Women

When, at his coming, we shed our robes
in the dust of the road at his feet
we thought it was a new gesture.
The wind grabbed the hem and the flutter was high.

It had been less brisk
when we undressed and hung in the cupboard
undressed and hung in the cupboard
our little potentialities, hand-embroidered,
hung them in a single confining fate,
generation after generation, female fate:
undressing, first by command and soon by habit,
our inherited ritual print.

But when he'd gone,
and our robes were rumpled
hoof-trampled bundles in the road,
and the wind allowed the dust to settle,
we admitted: it was all exactly the same.
We'd undressed ourselves ourselves:
all the half-finished tissues, all the soul's tangled wisps
yet again for the man, at his ass's feet.

Surplus Woman

No thanks, not for me,
any of that snug humdrum death,
mouse-faced fidelity round the pantry
(to cheese and the cat).

The stench of my used sheets
I'll keep to myself
and not aspire to sniff any others:

pay my personal bill gladly when it's due –
for this metre or two of silky sea
billowing around and embracing me,
for these well-aired sheets of clover, for a love
not glued to its own.

The coin I'll give is black night,
fabric that doesn't fade when the neighbour's door
opens a crack. I'll pay with an unappeased hunger
no smell of cheese can crumble.
I'll give my empty hand to definitive death in empty space.

Shirt

Made just one shirt. Not much good at it.
All thumbs, needle too thin
the thread goes kinky and grey,
don't know why.
The braided holes come out different sizes
all over the place, messy, don't know why.
Looks all right, though, from a distance.

He's sleeping there now, body blue
and curled up.
The shirt's clean, of course, washed first.
Looks very all right, it'll certainly do
for God:
   He looks from a distance, doesn't he?

from **ON LIFE** / ELÄMÄSTÄ (1972)

Pinafore

As I wake in the morning, you're still in my life.
It's not the moment of truth
but of grief –

made from the same plush as love:
velvet, dark and difficult to maintain.

Stripping it off, I put on a pinafore
and clear up the end of the day alone.

from **CITY IN WINTER** / TALVIKAUPUNKI (1980)

Crete

Some day without fail
we'll end up in the country of white light.
Grabbed by the scruff, we'll have our face
wrenched straight into the sun.
All the lines will face the light unreservedly.
Classical tragedy is pitiless:
no cloud allowed, no smoothing shadow:
it casts us, as if in bronze, in eternal age.

from **WAR OF THE ROSES** / RUUSUJEN SOTA (1988)

I'm in love with a rose –
those dozens of languishing eyelids
with no glances beneath.
A mere scent.
Zones of scent.
It's how I discover myself again:
all the tender surfaces – inner skin, outer skin, dead skin –
summer, an immense dead November too.
It's in me.
A blind scent.

(for Lassi Nummi)

Henriette invited us to have fish.
She'd left out the salt, or had she?
(Irma shook the cellar on the quiet.)
The tongue was baffled, hesitated, began to taste.
But yes.
At this mild kiss
the sleeping beauty of the senses slowly opens a petal.

When the poems had been put in alphabetical order
and the pocket hussars tricked out as princesses
(Margarita sat under the poems in her Velasquez skirt,
Maria and Karolina swung)
and the floor was scattered with roses,
there was nothing to do but dust.

We got sick of it and nodded off,
had nightmares for two hundred years
(even the princes had changed sex,
wouldn't kiss),
woke up one by one.
Someone opened an eye, her other bunged with tears.
The lovers looked away:
they'd said horrible things in their sleep,
emptied salt popcorn in each others' hair.

Maija went to get the paper
but the mice had nibbled it, or time had,
almost the door as well.
The books had let go their leaves too:
the poems were all anyhow –
they'd turned into new poems.
Riitta fetched a brush and started to sweep.
Kalle said, 'Swing – shall we? –
or just go back to sleep?'

TUOMAS ANHAVA

BORN 1927

KAI NORDBERG KY/OTAVA

Tuomas Anhava was the spearhead of the modernist revolution of the fifties, as both theoretician, translator, editor and critic, as well as poet. He discovered, among others, Haavikko, Saarikoski, and the prose writers Veijo Meri, Antti Hyry and Hannu Salama. It is possible to suspect a direct influence on Haavikko's manner, as Anhava's 'Once upon a time there wasn't a kingdom' shows.

He was drawn to both the stance and style of Chinese and Japanese poetry and prose: he popularised their economy and encouraged a spare, laconic, clean style in prose and poetry. His intelligent allusiveness and polished refinement are those of a miniaturist and imagist, but these limits contain a deep, critical and didactic subjectivity, working obliquely to enhance perception and enquiry. The poems are dominated by feelings of loneliness, awareness of death, love and a mysterious cosmos resisting conceptualisation. Yet these intuitions are contained within a strictly classical restraint.

His predilections are suggested by his important and influential translations of Blake's *The Marriage of Heaven and Hell*, of *tanka* poetry, Perse's *Anabasis*, Pound's *Personae*, and the poetry of Gunnar Björling and Bo Carpelan.

Born in Helsinki, the son of an engineer, he is Helsinki-centred and, like most of the poets here, urban, but like them he reverberates concretely to the archetypal Finnish landscape of lakes and forest.

He had the special distinction of being appointed 'Poet Professor', 1970-1975, an honour carrying the salary of professor without specific duties. 'May 1964', translated here, was commissioned by Helsinki University to be read at its degree ceremony in 1964.

POETRY BOOKS: *Runoja* (Poems) 1953, *Runoja 1955* (Poems 1955) 1955, *36 runoa* (36 Poems) 1958, *Runoja 1961* (Poems 1961) 1961, *Kuudes kirja* (The Sixth Book) 1966, *Runot 1951-1966* (Poems 1951-1966) 1967.

from **POEMS 1961** / RUNOJA 1961 (1961)

The moon of my youth was always thin and pale
stooped above the stars
                                        or collapsed on a cloud, exhausted,

now,
      any evening I go out
the moon's round,
                              the northern sky's ample navel,
                              slightly pulled in, slightly off-centre,
                              but girdled with lard against the cold,

and it never turns its back.

Once upon a time there wasn't a kingdom that didn't have a king and he didn't have a head.

It weighed heavily on him.

And he sought out a man who didn't have a spine and placed his head on the man's shoulders.

The king didn't die. Long live the king.

And he lived happily ever after, and the kingdom
endured for a thousand years and wasn't once upon a time.

from **THE SIXTH BOOK** / KUUDES KIRJA (1966)

A civilised regard, an educated voice.
Passes agreeable evenings.
In the company of good friends.
Drinks a glass of wine.
Knows the world contains everything –
the small, the medium and the large.

No one alive
   has ever seen him
except before a meeting or just after.

Trees, around-the-house conveners of wind,
bird-colonisers, crowned with smoke.
Forest, though…the only profile darkness has.
Flatlands: there, distance is a sound.
            An organising wind.

And the sea, the only portrait the sky has.
Darkness is quietly insinuating itself
like fingers up a thigh's inner surface
            towards the groin's soft cavity.

That expanse of sky, that square nautical mile,
that island, the lights, I've organised
all of them here for you,

I've laid in supplies of days, nights,
silence, noise, work and leisure,
I've been loading in supplies for ages –
nights, autumns, winters, springs, springs.

You give birth to boys (like trees).
I give birth too – I get you to bloom with my eyes,
and with my eyes
I bring a girl out of you,

and you take in all the aeons and the transitory world.

Anyone who believes what he sees
                        is a mystic.
In the dark walk slowly.

I've never made a book out of less;
I'll never manage to say more.
No one knows how to hope for his own birth,
and all the rest is speculation.
It's a land of flowing bridges.

from **POEMS 1951-1966** / RUNOT 1951-1966 (1967)

May 1964

I

May night,
night
of a day sunk in a western sea of May nights,
   a night mild with day's land-wind, ship-smoke,
   dim sails islands far stars in the masts,
   sky-shores,
the north
      bursting out of cold,
      a young man,
      a virgin,
      and a suggestion of tree's maidenhair, green, vivid,
      the earth wet and open,
time timeless,
      the northern night's high
      and unhurried high-flying peregrine falcon,
      quick as dusk, daydream,
      a moisture
      on the morning-and-city-pointing roads,
a gone May
            flaring the canted roofs
            in an ascending ocean,
youth
            with everything in its eyes, serious, green, grey
            and far-looking,
wind on the brow
and vanishingness
like a gorgeous ship.

II

Moments like statues, and a statue

    eyes blind with distance
    becalmed breath
    heartbeat marble under thorax
    stir of shadowless hand
    jewel of nakedness
    step of foot

categorical as dreams
unreturning as youth
who wouldn't find it beautiful to die in memory to be forgotten
for ever

when youth dies
we feel so immortal

III

Anyone young would go anywhere, do everything,
discuss whatever, meet others, always feel something,
and then sleep soundly the peace of this world.
So far he's not got the art of stiffening by heart,
the statue's or the starer's; eternity
bolts his spirit for a second, then the spirit walks on;
it's not on fire, but the flesh is alive,
wanting and fearing, one with the living;
whenever the sky flashes and the waters rise,
wind and vanishing visit his brow, crematorium-hot.
His pores are open, the world moves in and out
of the one who's young, the most alive, the most mortal;
our peace is constriction,
this certainty creates uncertainty, this dexterity gaucherie;
wealth impoverishes him, cleanliness muckies him,
and our shame makes him turn his head away;
work, so profitable, in many ways so unprofitable,
robs him of will; freedom, if granted, unsettles him,
and our dwellings drive him out.
Someone sees a peregrine, watches its fall into extinction.
Most watch us, but we don't matter;
Someone watches those who've reached the point of
not wanting anything, not even death,

the unclassified,
not numerous anywhere, but a scattering everywhere:
activity, the amount in our bones is harmless.
Who wouldn't fancy direction-finding like Youth?
That skilful radical, Middle Age, for instance,
the honest-to-goodness bishop at the PR meeting,
and Old Age, with its guide-dogs, Justice, Power, and Reality,
Belief, Beauty and Horror,
all the sisters of our dreams, and, always last,
Lukewarmness, the uninvited sister.
The spring, the sea, no living thing
unpoisoned! All of it in twenty years.
To the question what will happen the world answers
everything'll happen, truly everything.
That's something no one would like to wait for.
I grieve, the songs are dead,
I grieve for Scylla and I grieve for Charybdis,
each was a siren and each was stifled.

IV

I don't give a thought to the immortals.
I think about others, all the others
who can't be remembered, only thought about,
not imagined, only known.
The mortals,
more and more about them. *Manes et maiores*.
Their names only, if them. Dates, if them,
but years, years without end. The days gone by
with those who remember them, if any there were.

I don't see them as a procession, though,
an unspeakably sublime frieze.
Their ranks contain perhaps
  an old man fingering his illnesses like a rosary.
  A subnormal problem child being calmed with cold water.
  A nurse who told about it with a smile.
  A polite youth who employed a few choice words.
  Two women who read the paper from cover to cover every day.
Hard-workers the work-shy fidgety-fingered short greedy blonde
  once-bitten-twice-shy fly-by-night longbones.
Morning after morning night after night, that's how it is:
as you know, you can be buried in phrases.

Farewell
Goodbye
We'll certainly be along

V

The last day of May, of the last May
we won't see tomorrow
but May leafs into June
this morning a dusty pigeon turned its head and woke up
the day shone, you breathed blue air
the day shines the air's clear
and in the middle of payday, the middle of the daily reckoning
I come out of the bank
and I'm filled with awe at the great goings-on
filled with tenderness
women! women like perennials on the street
   men like walk-in cupboards
footsteps
the day's glittering, the cars are roaring
the trams the long-distance juggernauts the uncomprehending
   long lines of soldiers
If it's rained, where's the grove sending its scent?
what's the lie of that twig on the path?
where's the cloud going
when there's no one there, and what's blue?
I go in through the door,
the lift thuds and grumbles, the doors klonk,
the world's a city and doesn't stop, the flat's acquiring
      all the clitter-clatter.
What! doesn't stop: suddenly it's totally quiet –
      sometimes it is.
The flat gathers that in too
with its window open.
And then a blast: some lad's whistling: down in the yard.
Not a tune. Just whistling.

PENTTI HOLAPPA

BORN 1927

IRMELI JUNG/WSOY

The son of a foreman and a weaver, **Pentti Holappa** was born in Ylikiiminki, a village near Oulu in the North of Finland. This is a place of daylight darkness in winter and "white nights" in summer, but he has lived his adult life in Helsinki, and he early developed French interests and a corresponding cultural and political sophistication.

He has spent long periods in Paris: he was the arts correspondent there for a leading Finnish newspaper, *Helsingin Sanomat*. Later he was, for ten years, a political columnist for the same paper. Significantly, he has translated Robbe-Grillet and Sarraute among others, and in the sixties he was editor-in-chief of *Ajankohta*, an extremely influential forum for literary debate.

Politics and journalism have taken up important parts of his life. As a Social Democrat he held the post of Education Minister; he was Secretary of the Finnish Writers' League and has held other executive positions in cultural organisations and advertising. His poetry, however, centres on the heart and its difficulties, on the body and its complex and baffling situation in time and space.

His imagination shifts between realism, politics and the ecstatic – glimpsing possibilities of fantastic renewal in the everyday, since man is part beast, part human, part god – yet never losing sight of the restricting shortcomings of private and public life. There was a twenty-year break in his poetry, during which he explored the possibilities and tensions of liberation in novels and journalism. In 1979 he returned as a thoughtful, elegiac poet of passion and loss, yearning, frustration and occasional fulfilment. In a time of captivity, suppression, repression, disintegration and destruction, he sees possibilities of hope in the resources of love.

His spare and cleanly-written poems have become increasingly explicit, direct, realistic, and more popular in the process.

POETRY BOOKS: *Narri peilisalissa* (Clown in a Hall of Mirrors) 1950, *Maan poika* (Son of the Land) 1953, *Lähellä* (Near) 1957, *Katsokaa silmiänne* (Look in Your Eyes) 1959, *Valitut runot* (Selected Poems) 1977, *Viisikymmentäkaksi* (Fifty-two) 1979, *Pitkiä sanoja* (Long Words) 1980, *Vuokralla täällä* (On Lease Here) 1983, *Valaistu kaupunki ruijan pimeydessä* (City Lights in the Arctic Dark) 1985, *Savun hajua* (Aroma of Smoke) 1987, *Keltainen viiri* (Yellow Pennant) 1988.

from **SON OF THE LAND** / MAAN POIKA (1953)

Sower in the Wind

A sower in the wind is no knower,
the knower is flogged for his eyes:
his eyes have a soft passion –
the courage to look.

A sower in the wind has neither fear nor power:
for the sower in the wind, there's no sceptre:
his labour's casual,
and he walks away.

Off the Wing

Thunder cloaking the landscape:
a falcon's wing traces a cloud's edge,
and a hunted bird stiffens.
Their destinations are clouded by storm,
the falcon and the shy field bird.
A black fist steers them:
one up, down to the ground the other –
beats the falcon down to the ground,
the fieldbird up into the cloud.

from **FIFTY-TWO** / VIISIKYMMENTÄKAKSI (1979)

A flock of wings – waiting for you to come.
Open the door, and they flock out of my heart,
flourishing laurel round your head
and singing like silver.

You don't see a thing, just smile.

A million times it's happened,
and each time you stand there smiling.

from **LONG WORDS** / PITKIÄ SANOJA (1980)

Pain needs no armed outriders.
It stabs you right through, suddenly,
in person, as you sit in the bus.
Transfixed, you see autumn outside.
Every move you make, it starts to rain –
the landscape's misting, it's pouring down with pain.

A weird spring! Nothing but north wind.
May 15th, and not a bud on a tree.
Soon there'll be no room between two winters
for even the illusion of love, let alone the real thing.
But my heart's a straw nest,
fragile, jerry-built,
vulnerable to a climate such as this.

I ransack my mind for a person
to beg a little tenderness from –
just one thought, at the very least, to protect
a makeshift home against a rainy night
and a raw morning.

I daydream vivid eyes
and a body's casual grace.
All that's missing is a name I know.
The person forbids me to use it.

I won't acknowledge it – this flesh:
anaesthetised, dismembered, its
worn-down bones and stumps of teeth.

I walk alongside a man called me,
but little to see I could call familiar:
a flicker of childhood perhaps in his glance,
a warmth arrested on the riverbank –
otherwise walking foreign matter,
the lines on his palm not what happened to me.

Is this I that I glimpse in the cerebral paste
or the centilitres of spinal fluid?
The data are there: registers of pleasure and pain,
the nerves synapsed through the muscles.
The soul's there – call it the data-bank
where the stuff of experience is chemically deposited.
Here is how I'm inserted in the time-dimension,
not on my own, but like among likes, with
herds of reptiles, mammals and birds, where I wander
the winding corridors, backwards and forwards,
sifting the concept of infinity.

I stare inside.
I feel the explanation retreating
here, there, elsewhere, everywhere
and extremely close in a broadcast with no receiver.

from **CITY LIGHTS IN THE ARCTIC DARK /**
VALAISTU KAUPUNKI RUIJAN PIMEYDESSÄ (1985)

Seagulls in Autumn

Today's easier than yesterday. Weary, am I?
A sea contemplating itself, clouds in shrouds,
and two sails drifting away from each other.
Yesterday I was more in love with you.

Though I can imagine solar flamings through the clouds,
the thought of you's having a Sunday morning lie-in.
I'm breathing calmly, breathing like the sea.
The seagulls are taking soundings of autumn.

I could bear the smells of cold and loneliness
if the bright morning darkness
coming from your body and armpits didn't
tell me it's time to be near you, and wait.

You Would Be

If someone loved you
as much as I love you,
he'd not speak, he'd be
more taciturn than he used to be.

He'd not look, even if
you dazzled him lame and blind.

When shadows moaned about the street
at your absence, he'd know the pitch-fires
of torches that darken the stars at night
and the sun in daylight.

He'd not be himself.
Only you would be.

Torchbearer

My lover went out of me yesterday
and didn't come back even for the night.

My lover's walking somewhere bearing a torch,
encircled by darkness black as the dark in me –

the me I observe and see collapse to dust,
every particle with a sun inside.

Everywhere there are planets charged with night,
and in the night a torchbearer seeking perhaps despair's address.

from **AROMA OF SMOKE** / SAVUN HAJUA (1987)

Letter

Rain. A mouldering November
rots on the city roofs. Groaning ships
glut the harbour. Can't see the coastlines
of my life. I've no lighthouses.

Friend, you've not written, not
rung. From my mistakes, I learn –
as little as the shape of the water.
I yearn and my days cave in.

Under their umbrellas: old folk –
they hover, feet off the ground,
gesticulating: 'Don't dawdle!'
I see the dark at the end of the tunnel already.

The oldies advance towards the front line,
clear-eyed as water, a flickering
smile on their lips, and bolder than
war heroes on the pages of history.

from **YELLOW PENNANT** / KELTAINEN VIIRI (1988)

A Step Nearer

If existence and the chip of it called life
have nous, then it's fear and boldness,
boldness in spite of fear. I peep
towards awareness, to the point of blinding
by death. And still I piece together pyramids
from chance fragments, this by day,
that by night, and both crumble. I know it
and still I start. Still I love, even though
I've lost my hope a thousand times. I'm,
I know, each time a step nearer hope.

LASSI NUMMI

BORN 1928

JONKO KESÄLÄINEN/OTAVA

Born in Helsinki, the son of Lutheran missionaries who had spent much of their time in China, with one brother a composer and the other a painter, **Lassi Nummi** is both a prolific poet and a literate, sophisticated and cultivated journalist.

A leading critic of the visual arts, music, and books, he was for many years also the cultural editor of one of the main Helsinki papers, as well as the chairman of the Finnish Writers' League and P.E.N. For many years he has been the literary adviser on the Bible Translation Committee of the Finnish Churches.

For him poetry is distinctly an *art*, with an independent right to develop its formalities apart from any other purposes. Yet its organised recreation of the joys, passions and sorrows of moment-to-moment living satisfy a human need, a spiritual thirst. Emanating from people of lonely individuality, it is also the language of emerging consciousness and a tutor of consciousness.

He picks up sensations and awarenesses almost impossible to define: he is an attentive poet, with an acute ear; and yet the experiences he records, the scenes he observes, will be easily recognisable to many less articulate: he knows the beauty and strangeness of the normal.

His essentially religious temperament, always poised, it seems, at an outpost on the edge of vision, is checked and tested by an habitual scepticism and probably final agnosticism. Philosophically inclined, yet dismissive of all formulations, open to cosmic dread and horror and acquainted with mourning, he is also the balanced poet of sustained love. For all his sophistication, one of his most attractive facets is his uxorious, untiring adoration and enjoyment of his wife, which has resulted in some of the most enchanting love poems in recent Finnish literature.

He is conservative in the benign sense of wishing to conserve the tested good in an incurably evanescent reality; yet his title *Leaving Today* suggests a chronic awareness of departure and change, often accompanied by acute pain.

In 1990 he was awarded, as Anhava had been, the distinguished title 'Poet Professor'.

POETRY BOOKS: *Intohimo olemassaoloon* (A Passion for Existence) 1949, *Vuoripaimen* (Mountain Shepherd) 1949, *Tahdon sinun kuulevan* (I Want You to Hear) 1954, *Taivaan ja maan merkit* (Signs of Heaven and Earth) 1956, *Jostakin soi ääni* (A Sound Came from Somewhere) 1956, *Lähellä puiden latvoja* (Near the Treetops) 1961, *Kuusimitta ja muita säkeitä (Hexameter and other Measures) 1963*, *Hiukan valoa havupuilla* (A Little Light on Conifers) 1963, *Arpakuviot* (Random Pictures) 1966, *Keskipäivä, delta* (Noon, Delta) 1967, *Linna vedessä* (The Submerged Castle) 1975, Lähdössä tänään (Leaving Today) 1977, *Syvyyden yllä tuuli* (Wind over the Deeps) 1977, *Runot 1947-1977* (Collected Poems 1947-1977) 1978, *Heti, melkein heti* (Immediately, Almost Immediately) 1980, *Kaksoiskuva* (Double Vision) 1982, *Hiidentyven* (Weird Calm) 1984, *Matkalla niityn yli* (A Journey Across the Meadow) 1986, *Joulukonsertto* (Christmas Concerto) 1987, *Maailmaa, yhä: valikoima runoja* (The World Still: Selected Poems) 1988, *Karu laidunrinne* (Barren Pasturage) 1989.

from **I WANT YOU TO HEAR** / TAHDON SINUN KUULEVAN (1954)

When the world's over, I hold your small bony head,
and through sand my temples sense your caress.
That's how we sleep, and the pine-whisper is stirring
and the sand stirs and sleeps and caresses with white hands.
We sleep deep down through sand, and water and sand, and sand
down to the bottom of the world, we sleep down to the depths.
We sleep all the sand and all the weeping and all the sea.
We sleep the pines and the little house and the candle out.

from **SIGNS OF HEAVEN AND EARTH** / TAIVAAN JA MAAN MERKIT (1956)

from Chaconne

I've written a lot of strange poems on a lot of strange things.
Today I'm going to write a serious poem on a serious subject.
My subject is your ear. I've studied it, gone into it carefully,
researched it from all sides, in torrential light, in twilight
and outlined against grapevines in the half-dark, with you
talking, laughing, and silent, when tea's brought in,
at music, in uproar, or when everything's suddenly quiet
and the night wafts the far-off street through the open window.

Today

This tree is now so flowery
it's forgotten its twigs,
forgotten its roots,
it sighs:
'Take me, pluck me.
I want to speak to your eyes.
Oh, to meet someone and die.'

This flower is now so treelike,
it broke today – a day like a millenium –
into bloom, and it's lifting up
to the light
it's timeless look:
'Come – take shelter
in my sighing beauty.'

from **LEAVING TODAY** / LÄHDÖSSÄ TÄNÄÄN (1977)

from Leaving Today

Utter agony that you're feeling.
Utter peace there was on your face.
Longing like a pedal-point of pain, frozen in place
        when everything's living all around.

Today I noticed:
the land of death is not as distant as it seemed,
nor as fearful, and it's not black.

Why did I never call you apple blossom's sister
when you were still close?
Perhaps I was too shy. The words come now, with you
so far away before our eyes.

I wanted to meet those people, my friends,
chat with them.
You never said no. And not now.

I wanted to tell you about where I was going,
the country, its cataracts, its fells, its springs.
Now I wish you could tell.

Weeping is a hot spring sealed,
flowing down below.

Leaving today,
always leaving, always
on the way home.

Into my dream the chime
of church bells.
I waken to silence
to the lonely chirping of August's bird.
Through the open summer-house door
the glow of a rose, the lick of a poppy flame
against the dispassionate green lawn.
Bluebacked
apple tree branches
report a raw barbarian eagerness for life.
Oh yes, life is here. This.
And yes, life is elsewhere, other,
but today it's this way, sound and round
as a green apple
on a branch, on its own branch,
concentratedly pondering its own ripening.

The happiest moment of the day
in the morning, at noon and again with evening drawing in:
the stroll across the terrace.
Like love at second, third and again fourth sight.
The sea gives you an Etruscan blue look.
The tree by the door's an almond, leafing bushily.
The flagstones are white, thinly flecked and veined
like a woman's skin
who's not as young as she was
and someone still loves.

'The wind speaks.' If the wind really spoke
could we endure its words,
so void, so flinty, so groping?
Inside them
salt, horror,
mania: a long-drawn black speechless
wave that wipes the coast clean
of houses, woods, junk. It washes
your eyes. If I had some

feeling. Or thought. If
I were something. If I was I.
Gone.
There's nothing here. Only a draught.
Air moving backwards and forwards, soon to drop.

The pines, a crystalline ice,
truth.

Truth, how much more of a tangled growth
than youth knew.
No imminent mistletoe twig,
a trophy snatched in the valorous quest,
but the forest itself, and all its trees.
The whole tree
crammed to the needlepoint with death,
with life,
and is there a third name still...?
Timelessness? Invariance? Quintessence. Rest.

The pines, a crystalline ice,
and what do I catch of truth?
I feel the cold. I see the pines.

Three circles this way, five crosses that.
The methodological problem of how to be human:
living demands (seems to demand) action that works.
Action that works demands (seems to demand) faith. Faith
seems to call for a narrowing down, a cutting out
of alternatives. Honesty, and sympathy, love, joy
demand, seem to demand, a multiplicity of parallel alternatives,
thousands of flowers in every direction, a hundred
rollickingly promiscuous intellectual tracks.

A flower-meadow flowers, it's not much good
at being a cornfield. But it does manage its mission
as flower-meadow extremely well: it floods out fragrance,

allures the hooved and trottered kinds, bees, poets
to their useful tasks: accumulating honey, transporting pollen,
ruminating, writing poetry.
Let me
continue the comparison: a person too,
such as you, can be a flower-meadow
or a meadow-flower: which, you can choose yourself.
I, at any rate, am a bee.

Six poems from Macedonia

In the city of Skopje
where hillsides ooze melons and wine

in the city of Skopje
where September matures into must
like August's juicy fruit

in the city of Skopje
I saw a woman
who had hair, eyes,
and all the beauty earth incubates.

The words are an introduction.
They end. The poem begins.

Your face is so sad, girl.
Life has these masks,
they master us.
Sad today,
blazing with joy tomorrow,
dead the day after.

This luxury: cicada-song thronging the dark
against the waves' distant quiet rushing,
as the dim-silver configurations back
the ikons' medieval gold.

Long ago
in the dark grottoes between infancy and adolescence
life was a taste of lemon on the tongue.
Bitter

Long ago
in the sunscorched meadows
of adolescence stretching towards manhood
life was a taste of lemon on the tongue.
Piquant.

Then bitter again. Piquant. Bitter.

Am I sure any more if I know the difference?

I love the Macedonian girl on the bookjacket
   more than a picture
   less than a person.
I don't know if she's child, beast or goddess.
Complete beauty is scarcely beautiful any more.
   It demands a frame:
   the whole world, ugliness, ourselves.
When I love you, I love a person.
You're behind the worlds, and near, here,
you live like a landscape, you vanish into commonplace and rain
at sun-up you're born again
   before my wondering eyes.
You're mortal. You're not complete. You're beautiful.

I love the northern forests and the water and the northern sun.
I love you.

This is written on air and water, not stone.
On you, on you.

from **IMMEDIATELY, ALMOST IMMEDIATELY /**
HETI, MELKEIN HETI (1980)

As a man back from a long journey,
dropped asleep in the evening and waking in the morning,
doesn't realise at first where he's got to
and half-asleep, confused, eyes the things and curtains,
the door-jambs, the window dimmed to a rectangle,
and, disconnected, tries to find, remember, tries to remember
where he should be, go, whom talk to
and can't hear the children's voices, they've left,
and groping the intimate space where
in the night there was breathing, realises it's empty.
and, faces, places, rooms haunting his mind, rummages
for this place and, only half-knowing
what he's seeking, his wife's image, the image of his children,
finally, in deeper dread than ever abroad,
raises his head and peers closely at this outpost of the world

so I today raised my eyes and sought in your eyes
        our shared youth
and saw there age's empty room
full of the coming winters' severe light
which lingered a moment and then thawed
into autumn and spring,
the tremble of the first birch leaves,
a summer day's exalted stillness, where the curlew cries.

from **WEIRD CALM** / HIIDENTYVEN (1984)

Suddenly at five o'clock

Just as we were leaving the store
        for the slushy street
the red balloon fled from your hand
– though you've a hand
red balloons adore –
        and tumbled
        upwards
into the black waste of space.

Back at the cottage
it's quiet again,
complete calm.
Frost has pushed its roots
deeper into the dark.
Lights on in the house,
but no one in sight.
Long empty avenues to the door:
key on the nail,
the room as it was.
Through the window
those same motionless birchboles, three,
and the pines, also three.

The ice-surface of the lake
there, in the dark
is invisible, inaudible,
inaccessible to sense-perception,
not there.

This is no dream,
I don't think it is:
as far as I am in being
this desolation is,
this empty silence, cold, calm.

How futile all the inflation, joy, pain,
closeness, loneliness,
but to the trees, those three and three,
my lips unmoving, I say,

'Who'd believe?
Someone's leaving the city of light –
more a fugitive than a faithful sentry –
leaving, sitting in vacancy
and watching an hour in transit to the dark
as one of seven, at a sentry-post
at an extreme outpost of the world.'

What is its name? Thrush, blackbird
                                        or nightingale? –
singing in this spring night.
Fecklessly, recklessly – like a thing
all alone at the limit of everything,
yet every phrase this side –
something won for life.

Not much to add:
it quickens a feeling, and sets it free.
It is itself,
and absent, absent.
As if green night sang itself through the branches.

from **A JOURNEY ACROSS THE MEADOW /**
MATKALLA NIITYN YLI (1986)

So Often Leaving

So often leaving. Never there:
        just about to arrive
and simultaneously
gone, left behind, far off elsewhere
ready again
for the return, leaving

in the draught of dark on the icy sea
in the bright inside of a cloud
in the grey crush of a street
in a flash of time
travelling, travelling

Unafraid, calmly
let it canker your flesh.
It'll take you anyway.
When you're calm, open,
its image fits you. Its
   tremor of extremest light,
   of most distant darkness.

When you go to meet it. When
you let it root,
                    canker through you
a stabbing moment
you're implicated in it:
the prick of the root pierces your heart,
                    overhead hums
the vision of God. The universe.

PAAVO HAAVIKKO

BORN 1931

IRMELI JUNG

Helsinki-born and based on the city, the son of a businessman, **Paavo Haavikko** has published more than 60 titles over almost 40 years. These include novels, short stories, narrative poems with characters from the *Kalevala*, a thriller, collections of economic and political aphorisms, libretti (including *The King Goes Forth to France*, performed at Covent Garden, 1987), plays, TV scripts, and historical works, such as his history of the Finnish Steamship Company's finances and fleet during a hundred years of military and economic turmoil. He is also an accomplished businessman, investor and publisher, and recently, at 58, he founded a flourishing advertising and publishing company of his own. This learning, experience and expertise are the infra-structure of his mature poetry.

The carefully musical poems juxtapose love, death, sexuality, erotic politics, and the private and public worlds. His imagery leads the reader vividly, with often startling but intelligible shifts, through the ironies of identity, biology, love, commitment and lack of commitment, and in and out of possible worlds, in line with something resembling the 'Many Worlds Hypothesis' of physics.

Haavikko is disturbed by an informed, passionate, ambivalent, often cynical and despairing curiosity about power and history: how the world works. In spite of the pseudo-metaphysical dimension or at least concern in his work, he is belligerently anti-clerical and yet passionately if unsentimentally preoccupied with morality

– 'what is right or wrong, or right and wrong'. He has opposed all totalitarianisms, refusing to comply with fashionable solutions and compromises, and is not afraid of ironic polemic; and yet his awareness of the traps of language, particularly poetic language, can make his poems look like language games. He is in fact an "antinomial" poet, the poems forming dialectical sequences with theses, antitheses, but rarely syntheses. He is perhaps a kind of cosmic conservative, believing that man is inhabiting a history that does not, in essence, change, his cruelty endemic, let loose by attempts at reform, as by any shakeups.

In the late sixties he was made an honorary Doctor of Philosophy by Helsinki University. He was awarded the Neustadt International Prize for Literature in 1984.

A selection of Haavikko's poetry, translated by Anselm Hollo with an introduction, was published by Penguin in 1974 (together with translations of Tomas Tranströmer by Robin Fulton). This is long out of print, but Hollo has a new Haavikko selection out with Carcanet in 1991. There is an extended discussion of Haavikko in the Introduction.

POETRY BOOKS: *Tiet etäisyyksiin* (Roads into the Distances) 1951, *Tuuliöinä* (On Windy Nights) 1953, *Synnyinmaa* (Homeland) 1955, *Lehdet lehtiä* (Leaves Leaves) 1958, *Talvipalatsi* (Winter Palace) 1959, *Viisi runoa klassillisesta aiheesta* (Five Poems on a Classical Theme) 1961, *Runot 1951-1961* (Collected Poems 1951-1961) 1962, *Puut, kaikki heidän vihreytensä* (The Trees All Their Greenness) 1966, *Kymmenen runoa vuodelta 1966* (Ten Poems of 1966) 1966, *Neljätoista hallitsijaa* (Fourteen Rulers) 1970, *Runoja matkalta salmen ylitse* (Poems from a Journey Across the Straits) 1973, *Kaksikymmentä ja yksi* (Twenty and One) 1974, *Maailmassa* (In the World) 1974, *Runot 1949-1974* (Collected Poems 1949-1974) 1975, *Runoelmat* (Poems) 1975, *Viiniä, kirjoitusta* (Concerning Wine) 1976, *Pimeys* (Darkness) 1984, *After the deadline* (After the deadline) 1984, *Sillat, valitut runot* (The Bridges: Selected Poems) 1984, *Näkyväistä maailmaa* (The Visible Universe) 1985, *Viisi sarjaa nopeasti virtaavasta elämästä* (Five Sequences from a Rapidly Flowing Life) 1987, *Toukokuu, ikuinen* (May, Perpetual) 1988, *Rakkaudesta ja kuolemasta* (Of Love and Death) 1989. [This list excludes books purely of aphorisms, as well as his other writings.]

from **ROADS INTO THE DISTANCES** / TIET ETÄISYYKSIIN (1951)

Every house has many builders and is never finished
and history and mythical aeons are told over again.
Contradictory corridors lead to a glimpse of error
and a memory of the only time-immemorial –
which the rooms will mutter through to the end.

One day flowers will be grown on the abandoned steps.
A huge water main will burst and the gates will rust to,
        and a silver pool will spread.
Someone will marvel at the idiosyncrasy of the machinery
        and hunt around for tools,
laugh at a timetable and spend an epoch of a morning.

And I ride through charted lands,
        but the fowling hawks are being freed,
and I ride forward crouching,
        cape flapping,
riding ahead of the squadrons threatening their king,
        across fords and slopes,
hooves drumming under myriadmorphic trees:

I must ride from night into night
        swifter than the squadrons of thought,
squander myself responding to the fullness of days
        or throw in my hand.

from **ON WINDY NIGHTS** / TUULIYÖNÄ (1953)

Open house, and the guests coming.
Open wind, as you wait
aloof, in the cool.
And whom would you wait for?

The children's cruel games last till evening.

In the cemetery, this windy landscape,
under the stone pine,
here I turned, back down the path,
wind keening in the trees; I recalled the past,
yesterday's, the father of the the wind's mourning
for my mourning: that I was meandering here
not missing anyone –
no one missing anyone in this windy landscape.

from **HOMELAND** / SYNNYINMAA (1955)

Odysseus

Odysseus: I myself am ten suitors
in my own house, ten years have passed and the sea's black,
I'm ten suitors and I've lost the sea, it's another man's sea,
the sky's in my eyes always, the sky's jealous, like us,
the sky-walking reapers are jealous, not only of this land, but
of the sky that's empty: the sky of our thoughts.

Sea: the seafarer's close to the wrecking stars,
his brow bears copper, silver and hallmarked gold,
his voyage is cursed, never to arrive, his ship's the last,
we were jealous of his wanderings all the ten years
the land waited for his bones to rest,

there's sea, he has the sea, the sky
and Penelope, all this weighs less in the scale than his grief,
we were jealous most of his grief, the grief off his brow:
guests invited, all welcome, my house is loud with song:
I'm Odysseus.

What if success strikes us dumb, how can we endure
      without going dumb –
how without going dumb can we endure
      the established fact that poetry is nothing;
this is the glory of the current generation:
      we wrote the poetry and grow dumb,
listen, it's a time of drums,

      it's a time of drums,
drumming is a sound as if there were a hollow dumbness
      in front of the drums,
pure darkness that carries no sound

twice, no
seven times, the Black Regiment paraded here
      under their black flags,
and it's not the same, they paraded here but
      this is happening now, and only this time
is the drums' sound voicing this:

it's the time, it's the time before death, and before the trees
      burst into blossom, it's the time of drums,
this golden decade too has dawned and is setting,
      puny friendship is petering out, gold is turning to iron.

from **LEAVES LEAVES** / LEHDET LEHTIÄ (1958)

A squirrel scooped out of air –
                                        here
even the shadows inseminate the wind.

The books'll survive when I migrate,
the books, a drag when you leave,
unaddressed letters the wind shreds
and, once read, their leaves leaves.

Are spring, autumn, winter still in power, and that fourth?
They finger the slender stem before it flowers,
but what odour will conquer ours, not flowers, no,
we'll rise in the spring, but the world will be gone.

Raises her skirt, and rain rises, wind, the dark,
and when she's full and big, the child comes,
children, and with the children beggary,
and we have guests: rain, dark, beggary.

You marry the moon
and the sea, the moon and a woman: all deaf.
You can hear them talking, you can speak to them
and they say it's a game.

Li Tai-po, a Chinaman,
        craved the moon in the river,
                        fuller than the full moon.
And now he has it all,
            oars in the air, and an eye full of sleep.

WINTER PALACE / TALVIPALATSI (1959)

First Poem

Silver that I chase images into juxtaposed to make them speak.

The multi-gabled roof is clawed by the winds and the birds,
they're going north – the snow, the birds and the grass;
industry minimal;
                                        an aerial, an airy flourish or
an ear tuned to the wind;
                                        greetings and a goodbye,
tree tree tree after tree;
this is the song:

No time to see the green before it's gone,
and it was spring again, a bird tested its song,
and its voice was involved, involved;
                                                            vulnerable grass,
a house, a house with a man,a woman, a youngster and an oldster,
nine openings in the soul.

The spinning bonnet on the chimney's extension-flue
                                                    and three colours:
          green, black and grey;
melting snow, forest, reeds, a river and boats.
Fir, pine, birch, alders and a willow bush;
the nut grows tree-size here.

And it was spring again. The woman breathes into it
for long weeks, and it wails:
                                            I'm born, I'm a girl
and I'll go out alone and play round the front of the house.

Woodland birds, beaks at the ready,
and spring;
                                  all I can manage to say here is:

in autumn and spring plaster flakes off the wall,
   and snow, the birds and the grass go north,
or come from there and pass us by,
   and the clouds flake in the sky;
you couldn't call the sun naked;

did I say already, the trees and their branches,
  the willow too, grow bushy, the nut flourishes here?

The station platform blooms. As you march along,
  the whole universe clings to your legs, left and right, and
the columns are roped with creepers from floor to ceiling:
  this white city in architects' upright handwriting.

Would a little conversation suit here? How about:

  And winter climbed in the armoured car,
settled, lived out his time and went,
  the snow, the birds and the grass left us,
and winter abandoned his big galoshes and went north.

Is this one of the crossers of the Alps?

  No, no, not Hannibal, this.

Is it an elephant, then?

  No, no, it's a car.

But where's Hannibal?

  No, no, he's off on a trip.

Grab your hat with both hands, if you like:

the wind flicked the birds, the sea's rising, the trees thinning.

And in short:

  The old wing (1754-1762) is The Winter Palace
and as far as eye can see, the roof, the floor and
  the walls are straddled with Exalted Beings: Venus, Jupiter,
and women of full-bodied vintage.
  It's still observable that on the River Beresina
many lost their heads and their hats,
  that the Battle of Borodino was a victory;

this is what I'm on about inside my pate.

Second Poem

And I asked the way of the bird I am myself
    and the bird replied:

leave early – soon as the leaves burst out of night.

And when the newsleaf came, I folded it under my arm
    and crossed the square.
Exaggeration, of course! – but I picture
    it with fingernails broad as tortoises,
and I was walking towards this person who is Fear,
    his manners foreign-office, his memory absolute zero.

And I was matchstick-sized and I lit the paper
    to see through the rain,
and it was raining bucketfuls, and I crouched
    and I lit the paper with a match,
it didn't light, and I finally lit it,
    it flamed and the smoke flew,

and a terrible coughing came out as if someone inside
    had breathed in a flock of birds

and tinkle-tinkle, a bottle was tinkling there,
and there was going to be some Exalted Being in the bottle –
    it made me almost weep!
In the bottle – a being I wanted to meet,
    in the bottle!

And this Person was shouting and burning, in the bottle,
    poor devil, protesting,
and if it had a beard, it was burning, and if documents,
    the documents were burning,
and a horrifying fire was spreading from line to line,

and the bottle was swathed in newspaper,
    it was swathed in papers
like apple trees when autumn's coming,
    and It scrambled out of the bottle.

What a mad journey!

It hopped from stone to stone, from line to line –
    fifteen lines away
everything was in flames, it hopped, me asking:

    O say, Exalted Being, Flying Fox
      Where is the land that is not?

And It replied:

It is not. I was a rose and I began to swell,
    out of me burst the world,
and the shame makes me weep! To abort!
    I! A miscarriage!
And to abandon my world! No one knows me here!

That was the whole conversation.

It was a rocky walk along the shores of heaven.

Third Poem

I crossed the forest and called at The Winter Palace
    built 1754-1762,
I let The Exalted Being out of the bottle and It

    aborted! miscarried! flopped!
I'm on a journey to the land that is not.
    Ah, you, clambering on the statues,
Tourist! perhaps you don't realise I hardly
    recover my expenses on these poems.

I'm on a journey to the land that is not.

I picture a clearing there
    in an uncleared forest,
an emptiness bordered with forest, and I
    dangle upside down in the clearing
that is sky, I
    not keen on talking,
and not coming back, don't want to.

And my breath, I blew it out and left it mute,
    not to pollute the region with howling.

But as it happened I called my breath
back on loan to say goodbye,
and stole it, and that's what I'm carrying to
the land that is not,

out of this poem.

Fourth Poem

This poem intends to be a word-picture,
and I want a poetry that hasn't much taste,
and I'm imagining
I'm a thing with the longings of grass;

these lines have very little plausibility, for
this is a journey through known language towards
the land that is not,
this poem is to be sung standing
or read alone:

I also said that everything
is outside and I'm here;
I was dangling from trees like the birds do
and all the doors are locked open,
and I underwrite the passing day
unread, like a newspaper underwriting
the world's meaningless sheet, and I sleep while sleep wakes
and in sleep I say: I.

Thick forest, this,
scattered trees that are scared,
and in this forest
the voice is wet with sweat,

this is a landscape of burgeoning trees, and in here
the blind tree forgets its visibility,
it's hollow here and all the way here, the forest
burgeoned with flowers to shame me,

and should I compare myself to that unviable foetus
    it went so badly with,
the one the flesh would swallow, soft and tender
    and wholly female?

I didn't know what it was like to be, somewhere,

I wanted to be quiet,
I wanted to eat words and change
by necessity, as I was in fact born.

This is how far I've got:
                    the house in the centre,
at the table, attending to the pen, as far as the paper;
it's very northern here but I'm thickheaded,

and this is a poem I'm writing in autumn, at night, alone,
    and who is not I?
Here everything's ordinary. Here? - Here too:
someone who longs to be far away is loving the autumn here.

I in this poem am a mere image of a full mind
    who doesn't ask why the fruit-trees don't flower;
and who on earth could care about this luggage of mine
    and this mind I throw in for good measure,
floating in the air like a round ship, dawdling, windblown?

I crossed the forest and walked from line to line,

and as soon as you're born you can start peeping
    to see if there are stars;
my ungovernable greed looks sad suddenly, it poured with rain
    and what is poetry?
What I want to say is:
a small house, narrow, high, and the room I'm writing this in –
exaggeration!
            but I imagine it all happening,
and who's not alone and who is not a world?

I want to be silent about everything language is about.

I want to go back where I belong.

Fifth Poem

A beautiful child was playing in the sand -
    and writing with her finger:

    Who? where from? where to?

I replied:

    O beautiful child, tell me, is

She interrupted:

    I'm two children and I lead myself by the hand.

I asked:

    O beautiful child who have the art of conversation,
tell me where the grass-tree grows,
    where the grass flowers,
and the wind, and the wind's breath, the strawberry,
    the hay, the rose.

She interrupted:

    I'm having a row with myself
and I'm all contrary; I have conversations about everything,
    I'm a girl and a boy, one and two,
and are you night and day?

I:

I'm a poor thief, a productive consumer
    seeking work,
I want to go back where I was born,
    either/or or and/or
the outside walls can have vertical boards
    or horizontal ones or/or not –,
I want to be quiet there.

She shouted:

First calm the wind that's blowing and growing thick forest!

I:

O straightforward word-order, from which
there is only some occasional exception,
all the crookedness of straightness,
which is all-powerful!

She:

What do you mean by this praise of all-powerful language?

I:

I'd like to read the riot act to this poem I can't get out of:
      this breathing made trees grow –
I came through that forest there,
      but oh how it stormed,
            stormed like autumn.

That child:

But if it's so plastic, why shouldn't you
      try to get out –
go through the night and look for someone
      it would suit to a T,
waste breath?
      You should leave it
to one it suits.

Sixth Poem

And everything's ordinary here, except
      the thousand ships and the topless towers;
like a river to the sea
      I bring total darkness to the night,

this woman whose dress is blooming with unfading flowers:

      when the scent's gone,
she'll burst out laughing like a bad dream
      and smile with her teeth;

no, I'll pass her by, this one.

A woman longs to be blind as a mirror and undress alone;
    night, the passer-by, doesn't stop;
the woman who sleeps alone knows truly
    that summer is a cold country.

That's two women I've engraved on the night,
    but you don't fancy them,

I wonder if you'd desire the beautiful Helen,
in whose eyes Odysseus bathed,
    who complained that Troy
burned without warming, complained
that in this house you felt the cold in your bones

and what is the theme of this poem and is this a poem?

I'll bring out a woman who looks past you at you,
    a carnivore, a snare,
and a little meal that has a soft hunger –
    wouldn't she please you?

And she woke mildly in the middle of the night and listened.

What about this one? A tortoise on its back
    will always try to turn on its belly,
but this one won't. Wouldn't she like to be as beautiful
    as a rose closed up for the night?

And the woman rose from the bath, bent under her hair's
    weight and dried her hair,
and a pretty dimple appeared on her shoulder and disappeared:
    her limbs smiled.

Dreadful to be always on the move and end up living
    alone with an old woman.

There's no sad woman in the singular and, futile to stop,

everything's sad.

Seventh Poem

This poem is a short play, in which the year and the years
are a short line,
                                        and it began suddenly:

Under the overarching stars I'm fleeing poverty northwards,
I've abandoned the tower with its protruding ears,
this awful world in which visible images come out of ears,
this awful world in which a picture-voice comes out of eyes:

swallows flew from the shed's broken windows in my childhood.

O sky, empty orifice edged with dense forest,
O femaleness of the world!

        And Scene Two: on the riverbank.

Light boughs over the water,
        spring, autumn and spring and autumn
are the four woman-seasons the hand spread on the skin:
        spring rouged it, and autumn moisturises it,
winter is sleep, and in the summer her hair shone,
        and the mallards' creaking shuddered her skin;

soft is a woman's skin, when three unborn ones
        look out of her eyes,
and she has no name even for herself: perhaps

Dancing Caryatid, a pillar of the world that never wearies.

And this is Scene Three, in which this blooming woman replied:

I flew, I gave birth from flight

        and the world came,
this I'm supporting, I was the Flying Fox;
when there was no earth, no tree,
        I got tired:

I woke in the bottle and
I was small and the bottle tinkled
                                                            and I hopped,
I scrambled out of it and along the stones, I was
                                                                                    about to fall,

I wanted to abort! be empty! miscarry!
                                        when I saw
myself, who am the world.

I, broken like the windows.

And here begins Scene Four; she says:

How do I know what sleep is
    and where the shoulder ends and the breast begins?
Make this poem into an inexpensive winter home for me,
    with lots of cupboards,
and furnish me a room for the soul,
    and I'll live in this line a long time,
in verses that don't flake,
    a liveable voice, a house.

I:

This is Scene Four, and I'm contriving a poem –
                                        from what? from emptiness?
A short poem to recite standing up or lying down and alone,
and aren't you your house?

She:

How unsheltered I am, as a world: build the house at once!

I said to myself:

Don't pander to her, for what else do you want, and that's ruin.

And this woman asked:

    What are you muttering about?
Haven't you grasped that I want somewhere to live?

I:

I'll surround the house with the sun and the moon
    and points of the compass, up to four, and
near the house I'll plant trees, flowers, and a maple, with
    a hundred autumns on it already,
and the maple began to bud, to leaf and push out flowers, so
    I was amazed,

and this is Scene Four, and Five is already starting, I:

I too'd like to live in a house with my things, a large house,
and they want one word to be a complete sentence, they too hope
productive speech will survive;

I'm going out of this poem against my will,
I wouldn't like to get close to myself,
I'll let loose all twelve double volumes
of the history I've been illustrating,

and I'm going out empty from the fruit
that doesn't flower and is a poem;
a well-constructed sentence doesn't isolate me;

this is not a protest, I shan't discuss it; and I:

I'm walking through a poetry as open, closed as the decades;

and this was Scene Five; the Seventh Poem.
The play is over.

Eighth Poem

How can I get this tree felled
here in the middle of the plain
when it has to be sung down and I've no voice?
And what and who is it?

It's one of those beings, the tree,
that slept with a woman, till then a virgin,
with a shadowy Aphrodite-slit,
the rendezvous where the story started; it spread far;
everything's a dream.

Quiet now, and I'll come through the gates to meet you,
when the roses rise from the ash.

I'm moving away from between things and myself, and
I'm defeat, and I'm drawing near to myself,
whom I don't particularly want to meet,
or meet the grey man on the gravel road.
And who wouldn't be quiet under the pines when they're clouded?

This is a word-picture, in which everything is ordinary,
and I've tried many times without success;

an ungovernable equilibrium stretched the tree cloudward,
the grass was parted,
autumn probably, I'm polishing my money to stop it moulding,
money goes mouldy and stinks,
I lead myself by the hand, a child that's slow, towards myself,
who is coming towards me;
I'd like to say my say, since this doesn't pay,
I hardly recover my expenses;
here I'm totally in power, and the tree's in the cloud's,
the man's in the woman's; and the greedy poem
grew silent, swallowed enormous amounts as it grew silent,
and I'm drawing close to myself and I'm here already,
a walking plant, a cock's stride and a soul, with no children.

The most fearsome thing is Fear but I let it free,
and how it shrieked pricked by the branches,
and on one leg
it hopped like a crane in the garden – and why a crane?
A crane is shy of cold and was calling the trees to come.

And here are those few lines that had to be a list:

a round table-top, marble, one cast-iron leg, well-bronzed...
any old list of goods would do for what I aspired to,
but I didn't succeed
and I'm getting out of this poem:

and why should I try to write poems when I'm no Musset?

O, Mighty Satan, would not this seamy soul do?
All I ask of it is a little oakum caulking
to make me look more ship-shape.
I'm not at home in this uncommercial world
and I pledge this soul if thou wilt let me sail
free of charge past the lighthouse;
O Ancient Gentleman, Lightbearing Spirit Rich in Ideas,
O Hands Filled with Torches,
take not amiss this almost insolent offer
recalling the past:
thou deemedest lucre was filthy. And thou knowest.

O Prince, I am one of thy men and thou canst
      afford to let me go.
Hast thou not got others to uphold thy voice, who
      turn up regularly, unlike me?
And I'll take in hand thy affairs elsewhere.

I know that money arouses not thy lust, and that
      thou desirest children to play happily;
O deliver me from this place, I've deserved it
      and I'm not at home here;
I'm not at home in this uncommercial world they've contrived.

And where would I squeeze in when the Rose is growing?
      Too cramped, this Palace, to turn in one's sleep.
What World could house two Stories –
      greedy stories, not satisfied with Scraps?
It's cramped in the Sea: too cramped for a couple of Fishes.
      Everything is impossible.

Ninth Poem

And in sleep I'm always in a tree I see
      at the equinox, autumn in the land,
and through the eyes flew a flock of birds,
                                        warm yourself
      when the puddles ice over, here at the bottom of the sky,
the sky's thin and won't hold up, and the soul's at large.

from **THE TREES ALL THEIR GREENNESS /**
PUUT, KAIKKI HEIDÄN VIHREYTENSÄ (1966)

from The Short Year

The one who writes us is now doing four plays a year.
But the flowers fall in the summer more, and autumn's
a rich old man who can't see the limit of his resources:
empty rooms, unheated.
Spring's a flutter of shrieking birds,
and even shuttered windows don't stop them piercing the psyche.
Shrieking birds, the black-throated grebe.
And a love that goes smoothly is a dream.
Winter: this play's to be played out in the dark,
which alters the voices;
its light in the candles enclosing the chrysanthemums
is for you. We go with open eyes, seeing nothing,
groping with our fingers.

I light the candles each side of the winter chrysanthemums.
I see you, your fingers splayed, counting on your fingers.
I know what you're counting: the months.
Soon you'll talk about it.
The fingers that make you a door are now
occupied so abstractly.
A short year, so short that at the year's end
you'll be hugging a three-month baby;
or like a man's life, a year, and the second snow
has already fallen without his making a single print.
Death comes abruptly to a man. A woman makes her death
little by little, makes children,
and her happiness is to die before they do.
When she weeps for a child, her voice and her flesh are one.

My grandfather, the Emperor, was, as you know, mad,
wrote poems in the presence of others.
You want war,
it's available.
You walk stiff-legged,
like soldiers do, hysterics before an attack.
Hysteria is an illness that never gets better.
The hysteric is a winner, he never gives in.
No use my talking. I'll read his poem:

The mist is so dense, the water's hidden from the bridge.
The flowers are having fits,
as they have
to die so nonsensically.

Trees, nights are little by little a little longer,
a little, not enough to notice.
And the dark doesn't diminish the swishing in the trees.
Still, it's sad as a child
you speak to calmly, concealing something,
though he knows already.

In this cruel world it's useless even to beg
not to be born again.

When women have become pictures on the walls,
men shadows
walking beneath trees,
conferring on perversities –
being reborn, not dying, resurrecting –
the tree-shadows on the ground, on the snow, are brushwood.
One of them would like to saw it up.
Impossible, say the others.
He's not convinced.
Every time they walk beneath the black
they dread a snap. It doesn't happen.

As when snowfall again reminds you of something
    you can't quite recall, don't like to ask about,
if I told you it straight out
        you wouldn't understand
that I love you.

And she moves in a room of nothing but waiting water,
    moves as if the room were full of mirrors,
making it meaningless to try anything
    because of existing in every direction.
She grows quite calm, as if there were no mirrors,
    or they were blind, like a masseur.
She wanted to see herself without looking – she could try
    if there were only one mirror.
And the air has breathed all her skin's perfume
    without realising, as if it were asleep.
She keeps the light on unnecessarily long in the morning –
    she's alone in the room – to stop the dark
abruptly going out, but does it intensify the pale morning moon
    when a child's paper dart sticks in the grass?

You're a long clause.
No one could claim you've not got shapely knees.
Have I ever said it's important to me?
No one could claim it's like sitting in bed,
        grabbing a grasshopper
    and not knowing where to let it go.

There are people whose feet, one could claim,
    don't quite fill up their socks.
You get uneasy, and go quite stationary.
You don't primp the lie of your hair,
    though your hand would like to.
You hear things. I see them.

I prefer a slowness in things like the dark coming in November,
 how things recur –
 those don't, do they? –
and what we're doing here, something formal.
 The candles go out when the dark does.
You start dressing by undressing.
 The water wakes.
You finally throw out two corselettes.
 Time of the waning moon.

Nights are long just now,
 short though
 when twilight is on the skin
and someone's breath is mingling with someone's hair.

Leaves want to dance, and they get wind and storm,
 and autumn days, suddenly calm, and open;
and if the pines started to shed needles
 you'd not dare query was it always so every autumn.
Nights. As only softness can be cruel,
 her soft childlike features are showing
a furious face. Her names are Nightbeauty,
 Softness, Always, Two-Shallow-Hollows,
Dimple-In-The-Pelvis-Just-Above-The-Thighs, and
 Two-Just-Near-The-Spine, as if someone had
just pressed them there with his hands,
 That-Smiling-Absentminded-Look,
The-Look-That-Comes-When-A-Hand-Is-Drawn-From-A-Glove.

You can be certain that it itself,
not another,
no one else,
has been introduced to you,
the world itself:
it's not some allegorical creature
celebrating ancient rites,
and that's why you couldn't quite catch its name,
for it talks confusingly fast
and about everything at once.

It's a risk, using this handwriting
that might not be readable in the morning.
When even the snowfall reminds me without avail
of something I can't remember.

Warmer than the air around her,
cooler than the waiting water,
she dawdles long, alone in the room,
without dressing,
as she's nothing to take off.
Awful to see such great despair, so few gestures.

There are many sages, but on the other hand not one
stupid tree.
After writing the most difficult thing
is reading.

from **POEMS FROM A JOURNEY ACROSS THE STRAITS /**
RUNOJA MATKALTA SALMEN YLITSE (1973)

from Poems from the House of a Novgorod Merchant

The male seeks himself, woman, God, the tribe, age, the grave.
    A seeker, unappeasable by less.
Twins, half a person, a single fate, firm proof
    that a person is composed before his birth.

Woman, dreamstuff, meat that's sweet,
    spun manically, hastily from dusk,
to be done when the dream brings the male,
    knitted from twigs, gathered from the wind, fast walking.

You don't want what you desire, says the dream.
    Bad dream. Punish it. Get it out of the house.
Harness it to horses and gallop it off with horses.
    Hang it. It's deserved it.
Feed it with mushrooms, poisonous ones.

In dreams overwhelming armies are maintained at small expense.
    Fear ten thousand; hatred a hundred thousand.

I dreamed of a man who was out to do me in a deal.
    Out to give me counterfeit money –
a counterfeit king's counterfeit money!
    But luckily for me, my goods are rotten,
rotted in transport. He was blind with greed
    and snapped them up, the goods.
Rotten money for rancid goods.
    Not a bad deal for me.

For better a pig in a poke than bad stock
    that nobody wants.
With bad stock, you can't go to law, seek justice,
    but with a criminal merchant you can.

So alone. That, as the only jewel
                on her breasts,
    she raises her arm, scratching her neck.
The hand is someone else, the neck someone else's.
    Self-deception.
She, her hand, arm, breasts, throat, neck and her scratching
                are an intaglio depicting
that a woman suckles not a child but a fate.

from In Praise of Investment

When bones are crushed. When tendons are cut. Blood is shed.
    When the entrepreneur cultivates pepper in the mountains.
When saying that the enterprise is under way and it is
    is a crime. Worse than critical ability.
It shows there's no conception how keenly the Gods
    and their adherents are intent on preparing a delicacy:
black pudding. That's why the pig is putting on lard.
    The ingredients are being gathered: choice ones.
Blood, giblets, lard, pepper and salt.

The Gods, who eat the best bits as dainties,
    say that, fresh, it's delicious.
Whoever said that power tasted no good didn't know:
    those who know know it's a dish of dishes.
Casseroled, a little shallot, a touch of pepper –
    it's like the finest cuttlefish, or oysters.
Discussing it, many a god has been caught out,
    snarled in his own connoisseurship –

swearing these dainties are mountain-delicacies,
    though he swallowed something quite different.
That's why the people's darling dictators are short on brains.
    Look at them carefully: after the long day's work,
they rest in the grave, heartless, liverless, brainless.
    Political Science can't explain it.
This too is referred to Plato or Aristotle, who
    always return a uniformly wise reply.
One point never, though, about the adored dictators,
    that the people loathe the one they love.

Mystified, I read a writer who in his time
    didn't resist the system of his time.
Mystified, I read a writer who endorses it today.
    The dictatorship of the General Good.
A horrible sweet dream sugars the general tedium.
    Those enduring this blight
bless their luck that they spent their youth
    under an autocracy. Children,
the horror of that I've no words to portray.
    And you'd burst out laughing.

I'm afraid you chose a job promoting exploitation.
    Quite a few mitigating circumstances, though.
Inside the job, you're a flower in a fruit.
    You're inside its mask, and busy.
It seems rugged inside, and the eyeholes are minute.
    Outside they may be throwing stones.
I understand you. Listening to how our different ways
    brought us to the same file in the chain-gang.
A common understanding unites us: rulers
    have in truth very little room for movement.
The state's an edifice. When we ask room to move for ourselves,
    they call it calculated lateral deflection:
a crack of a millimetre down here –
    and it's a metre up there.
The building's so high.
    It's not easy for them.

Under the new order inflation is no longer tolerated.
    Money is the people's and has their name and stamp.
Talk of inflation is a punishable offence.
    Because it's been stopped.
And verbal provocation of devaluation is prohibited.
    The unfortunate at my side claimed
the government was again enhancing the price of goods.
    This unfortunate was sentenced
for his indiscreet pronouncement to isolation
    for a long-term period.
For as long as the sequestration of the workers' money
    for investment, banking,
and in general more considered uses shall continue.

from **IN THE WORLD** / MAAILMASSA (1974)

I vote for spring, autumn gets in, winter forms the cabinet.
Tell me whose lot you stand with, whose songs you sing
    with your mouth full of glass.
I'm against socialism, capitalism, its, their crimes.
I'm against their crimes, I swear, I share in them.

The best of man is his short duration,
            that he disappears
  once and for all.
Dead from the world's foundation
            till his birth,
  why should he wake up to do things
that'll last for ever?

When the bad lady wants your promotion, colonel,
    she wants you posted – after your house, general.
When your TB's getting terminal, it's lysol for you
    as your cough mixture.
A man a dictator only saved with difficulty
    from his own oppression
became a showpiece people came miles to see.
    Drowned himself.
A woman who rushed with her children
    onto a Jewish extermination train
left nothing but ash, colonel, ash and a widower.
    A man who refused to tell the story to the end.
He was eliminated. Look around you. Why should I go on?

In debt for goose eggs, don't take a loan for duck eggs.
When the rate's ten per cent, it draws gold down from the moon.
When they're buying, sell. Buy when they're selling.
First think slowly, then act quickly.
Get out of bad businesses fast.
    Forget them.
A hundred years from now this is a hundred years ago.
Never be afraid of the obvious.

The seedlings, the firs, need your help through the grass.
  For a year or two, perhaps five, they're grateful.
Then the grass needs your help to survive the trees.
  It goes bald round them,
                around their majesty.
And the pine that grew fifteen years in an alder grove,
  three feet high, sinuous, bowed, bent with snow,
      starts to prosper.
It kills everything within reach
  for the next two hundred years, annually.
That's where it has to be.
  Never say it's growing in the wrong place,
      a tree.

Not the supposition
        that we're going somewhither,
    but the supposition
        that the river stops, curves back, stills, stares back
    at where we stem from, back,
that if life were a river you'd
    weep on its bank.

from **DARKNESS** / PIMEYS (1984)

Days become years. Years
        become places. Then you must go.
Thirty-three years. Said three times,
        it makes a hundred. I can count.
But I don't know if the door out
        opens out or in.

When ass's milk has turned to cowclap
    a miracle has occurred.
You can tease a tree or a person,
    not kill a frog.
You can cut an image in a birch, oozing sweetness,
    undisguised, unconcealed.
You can lash a fir, lacerate its back.
    It doesn't moan. Doesn't dare.

Windy drought. A southern damp contrives
    a blue. Many a blue backs the columns of the economy.
A dead fieldfare sprawls, wings spread,
  three bees feeding at its torn throat.
I bury it, with blessings: So long…
Who knows where animal souls go,
    deep down below
        or up high.

from **FIVE SEQUENCES FROM A RAPIDLY FLOWING LIFE** / VIISI SARJAA NOPEASTI VIRTAAVASTA ELÄMÄSTÄ (1987)

Sounder deeper sleeps the man
whose blood has
resolved into writing

You can't take it with you – even the mite
they stole from you
No use jingling shillings in Hell

Mix might and water:
it's wine –
Alcohol Poison.
No miracle in wine

Politics, the art of the possible
made finally impossible

Grant O Lord a day of eternal life
A temporary millenium
One day nearer
The death and destruction of the superpowers

The soul attacks the state,
crack willow the gaol.
No, that grows by the wall,
sentenced for life,
by roots, outside the wall,
a living shade.
The soul attacks the state,
crack willow the gaol.

from **MAY, PERPETUAL** / TOUKOKUU, IKUINEN (1988)

After ten springs in the same slush
        the cock crane knows he's eternal
                                        as marriage.
Knows not a whit about the world.

Finally the casualties pour like rain
                                incessantly.
        But the Samurai raises no umbrella.
    They pour into the heart.

Before birth and after death
    in God's sight and out
you're priceless as in your life.
    He doesn't love or hate you.
He's no monkey or model.
    Choose Him yourself, from nothing,
and make Him in your own image.
    It won't change him, or diminish.
He's the sacrifice of his sex.
    He's a woman.

1

Unslit, unopened
    burnt letters.
Stop malice, madness
                            and meanness,
        three sisters whose father
is envy, at my stoop,
                                on my steps.

2

Nothing goes as planned.
Everything goes.
You don't get a grip on your life,
because it's a barney;
life gets no grip on you,
on me, and never will.
It summons the bouncer,
whose grip is brief.

3

Respect, a good name,
a placid pride.
A good name has no price.
It's only to be spent,
not bought.
If ever for sale
it has no value.

4

Age enters the garden.
Now I see my defeats
coldly
as steps, gates and a road.
Young wine maddens.
Old wine is wise.
Here someone ages
and toddles blind
round the puddle.

5

Poetry is no season
or weather:
it's a climate;
no place, no landscape but
an all-purpose economy and history
in a single house.
A passion larger than life.
Masoned so that however many
it's masoned from,
it shows no seams.
The seams are all in sight,
the different stones one slab.

6

The colonial goods are coffee, tea,
sugar, cocoa, spices,
fruits and grapes.
A colonial country means a developing country,
developing means rape and robbery.
Developing is a good word, it develops.
A developing country's name is really
Colonial Country.
Developing companies' names are
Stick-in-the-mud, Stupid.
A holding company has two faces,
paper-thin, facing each other.
Holding means Black Hand.
A holding company's names are
Brazen, Brass-necked, Sick.
Slowly, Sneaky and Security
are investment company names.
The Bank of Finland's name is the Bank of Finland.
The Post Office Savings Bank is getting a new name.
I'll go and work there when I grow up.
When I graduate, I'll be a stockbroker.
A stockbroker is a middleman:
two people remaining unknown to each other,
he's paid to buy stocks from one
and sell them to the other.
The Helsinki Bourse has one stockbroker.
There's no other in sight.
The Bourse's logo has been stolen.
Not stolen from it, it stole it.
Who's it? No, not the Board of Ethics.
But everyone except the one concerned
can easily recognise the party
that remains unrecognisable to the other party
because it is itself it.
It itself is the stockbroker and the buyer and the seller
and there's the crime and that's the profit.
It's called the Bourse, but
it's not it yet.
One stockbroker is inadequate to make
a Robber's Den a Bourse
except in this Eastern European sense.

Nevertheless there's one stockbroker more
than in the Moscow Bourse,
just as many chairmen as in Moscow,
just as many speeches.
For it's a Robber's Den, you see.

7

When a person writes he may end up
short of money and food.
A publisher is in danger of losing property:
call him a bookmaker
with dodgy days at the races.
But when you're writing and notice
the cold pinching your fingers,
you've forgotten to light the fire.
If you've got dry wood on your hands,
autumn evening's welcome to come.
It does come, showing forth like fire, or a spirit.
Poetry is passed down
from generation to generation like yeast,
raw and rude.
But it has other qualities too,
quite a few.

8

They've not all got hair
and they're not all women;
so there's nothing to cut,
no hair, not even a bald man's baldaquin.
No, they're not women,
but not men either.
An opportunist is born a god,
an hermaphrodite, serviceable
to himself at all times.
A parasite survives the corpse of the host.
They've served Hitler and Stalin,
but how did they manage
to bow to both, but why not?
They've earned their pension
but not a grave.
The judge is a humanist, the executioner a technocrat,
but this crime is unnameable.

  False witness in a waste of time,
bribed bulletins without a bribe or gift.
  So multifariously ungifted
as always with crime.

9

What I long for most is a circle and a square
  and a caterpillar track, and the day's rates too,
but not education.
  No one educates you for this,
neither first nor last.
  Because it can't be learned, one's got to
      know bang off.
All the tritenesses, like the way of all flesh,
  come true.
I hate goodbyes because
  world-without-end goodbye means
    meeting soon, over again.
The great system of conceptions, bankrupt
  and a booby, like the rest.
And above all maybe what one can't even be
      bothered to say.
    What's the use of haggling?

10

When the soul seizes power,
  the mind makes it its heir,
imitates a musical box
  itself always listening
    and astonished
that a mechanical nightingale has
  a nightingale's lot,
    a marsh warbler's:
      to concoct, echo
  and coax the whole clutch of voices
      into its voice

MIRKKA REKOLA

BORN 1931

IRMELI JUNG/WSOY

Born in Tampere, the daughter of a newspaper editor and a teacher, **Mirkka Rekola** lives in Helsinki and sets poems there, but her Zen-like perceptions are most at home by the Finnish lakes.

For her the world is a continuum, experienced, as Confucius or Lao Tzu might experience it, as an unfolding process. She lets her language abrade the distinctions and boundaries drawn up by rational consciousness. All permanent-looking statements about the world are false, all antitheses misleading.

Re-enacting the ancient mystical pursuit of Oneness, she experiments with statements that shift their appearances, as in optical art, according to the *gestalt* of the reader. In the resulting laconic musical confections, impressions tumble out, often in apparent disarray, but recording tenderly remembered moments in the mind's own spontaneous order. She writes, not philosophical poems, but minutely attentive wistful narratives. She also writes collections of aphorisms, and her poetry is strung with aphorisms.

She is difficult to translate convincingly, for much of her effect depends on nuances and ambiguities of both word and feeling. She is the kind of poet who implicitly invites the reader to enter into the creation of the poetic occasion.

POETRY BOOKS: *Vedessä palaa* (It's Burning in the Water) 1954, *Tunnit* (The Hours) 1957, *Syksy muuttaa linnut* (Autumn Changes the Birds) 1961, *Ilo ja epäsymmetria* (Joy and Asymmetry) 1965, *Anna päivän olla kaikki* (Let the Day be Everything) 1968, *Minä rakastan sinua, minä sanon sen kaikille* (I Love You, I Tell Everyone) 1972, *Tuulen viime vuosi* (The Wind's Last Year) 1974, *Kohtaamispaikka vuosi* (Rendezvous Year) 1977, *Runot 1954-1978* (Collected Poems 1954-1978) 1978, *Kuutamourakka* (Moonlighting) 1981, *Puun syleilemällä* (Embracing a Tree) 1983, *Silmänkantama* (Eyeshot) 1984.

from **LET THE DAY BE EVERYTHING /**
ANNA PÄIVÄN OLLA KAIKKI (1968)

The nights are no longer warm,
the blackcurrants taste cold,
the muskrat's swimming faster,
the city lights are thickening.
The spruce rocked its top over the roof.
I can't shake off the thought
that something's been forgotten.
Drumming of a train in the east, owl hoot in the south.

The name of the quilt is limewood gate.
Whoever creeps under it sleeps
a deep blue dream all autumn

and is a hand under the pillow,
they're a hand under the pillow,
their heart a valley of echoes.

You'll never get such tenderness
ever as from the snowfall's
thousands and thousands and thousands of moments.

Sometimes I put this notebook down on my stomach.
The shiny black cover darts a speck of light
now on the wall, now on the window.
On the wall and on the window.
On the wall. On the window.

from **I LOVE YOU, I TELL EVERYONE** / MINÄ RAKASTAN SINUA, MINÄ SANON SEN KAIKILLE (1972)

My parents were anxious to sleep
when, as a child, I told them
their bed was speeding through space –
you could see the stars tiny in the window
and their bed speeding along the pane.
They pulled the clothes over their heads
and turned their backs
like the earth wanting a rest from the light.

from **THE WIND'S LAST YEAR** / TUULEN VIIME VUOSI (1974)

She's sitting at the table where I sat
and watching the street.
        Spoon in the coffee cup:
a tinkling like the halyards on the yachts
just now in the shore wind.
I'm thinking of going, or am I thinking even that?
I never meet anyone I know here now,
is anyone left
is anyone leaving?
Even coming they were going.

Those who wander around unremembered
sometimes ask,
Have you seen me recently?
Lost everywhere – everywhere –
because in them the whole world's
losing its mass.
I saw their yearning in all its actuality,
and it was I, broken like that,
always a stranger here, always as if at home.

from **RENDEZVOUS YEAR** / KOHTAAMISPAIKKA VUOSI (1977)

The yard walls are sinking under snow,
soon the trees will too,
        the streets are getting blocked, the cars
are whitening,
    the snowploughs are grumbling, and the shovels,
there's no human speech
                    to speak of,
even I know nothing about you.
Last year too went by,
                        my old father
no longer peeps out of the Peter Street window,
he's gone.
Do you think there's still time to grow old?

from **MOONLIGHTING** / KUUTAMOURAKKA (1981)

As long as I thought
there'd be someone else
        to eat with you, to sit opposite you,
it was better that you didn't come.

When you carried that rug
                  in your arms that autumn,
there was not a bit of wear on it as yet.
'Lovely art-nouveau colours, look,'
                                                  a new rug,
hugged in your arms,
not long; a small hall, a short floor.
When you were embracing it I
                        almost felt it was breathing,
that rug, it breathed that autumn's colours, and this one's.

The child at the opposite table
looks across this way.
                        What can he see
behind his back, in our window?

from **EMBRACING A TREE** / PUUN SYLEILEMÄLLÄ (1983)

Driving through rain with you
                    in a sea of rain
all I could see were the bridges, the bridge-balustrades,
                the overtaking lanes,
when the earth rose into my eyes
I heard, I heard I was in love.

Coming down the road through the forest
it's so steep
the fir-tops are watergreen,
                    green water,
as if it was all just beginning
I feel my knee against yours,
                        the windscreen's
steamed with breath, yours and mine,
do you think, sometimes, in town, its windows…

At night, hearing my breathing in you,
and your skin warm under my hand
                  I see in a cloud of colours,
your right shoulder
mottled by lake-reflected midnight sun,
                      my childhood, in a new alliance,
shore and water, and the water risen,
and I didn't want to make it up the hill, I did make it,
and then I was in a blue atmosphere,
                        a boat in my eyes,
I raised my hand, and the water, it was still rising.

At first I thought it was just rising.
I saw the steeples, there were two,
double windows then and at least two, eyes.
It was on the stairs, it was on the stairs when
I felt you on my lips.
I'd have still waited for you even in the doorway.
And as a door. They were double doors.

I raised my hand. It's between hands,
it's between hands here,
so that I go through gates of memory and I want.
So that I want to see my heart as a person.

Have I stripped you of memory,
                                        of memory you –
created by caresses, a seaworthy rock in my lap.
Sun, and sun
in my hand, I through my years,
a tern-plunge into water, ah, ooh, and out –
even the waders
find each other in these waters.

What floats you
                  sinks you too,
the tree's on the water's arm,
and the water on the tree's.

Embracing a tree we grow.

When the maple was blooming there
I lost time
at least twenty years,
less than the maple's age,
                     a new heaven and a new earth,
when you were there, I straight away felt you behind my face.

All over town there are
                                    maples,
last spring leaves even sprouted from the trunk,
I'm waiting for this tree to grow
into shade for my hot room,
each spring it stretches up its top,
                              its blossoms
are in the window already, its window
on your eye-level in this town,
                              from this height
it's a single tree, from below there are many.

SIRKKA TURKKA

BORN 1939

PERTTI NISONEN/TAMMI

Sirkka Turkka was born in Helsinki, the daughter of an army major and a chancery clerk, but pursues her freelance career in the wilds. She has been an agricultural trainee and chief stable manager, and her close rapport with animals, particularly horses and dogs, is reflected in her poetry, with its felt physicality and emotionality.

Her intensity is occasionally agonised, though her sharp humour is seldom far away and gives her tone its distinctive tang.

In mourning, her flow of strong bitter feeling leads to an incantatory *duende*, gathering up impressions of nature and transfiguring them into what seem substitutes for cries. A very concrete, intelligent and humorous mind controls these keenings and is very conscious of the figure it cuts, its uniqueness and its right to exist as an eccentric individuality and survivor. In love, and in less extreme situations, she plays with an almost clownish, sad-faced persona as a metaphor for genuine and profound upset, creating a literary presence of great clarity and charm.

In 1987, with *Come Back, Little Sheba*, she won the Finlandia Prize, an annual prize on the model and scale of the Booker, but not confined to fiction, and first awarded in 1985. Her book has a caste of animals including a crane, a tiger, a wild boar, a cheetah, a donkey and a favourite cock: the book contrives to be a love poem and an imaginative history of evolution at one and the same time. There are black moments in the sequence but it is on the whole a perky, cheerful, entertaining and witty treatment of anguish.

In 1990 she was selected as the poet on the International Writers' Programme in Iowa.

POETRY BOOKS: *Huone avaruudessa* (A Room in Space) 1973, *Valaan vatsassa* (In the Belly of the Whale) 1975, *Minä se olen* (It's Me) 1976, *Yö aukeaa kuin vilja* (Night Stretching Like Corn) 1978, *Mies joka rakasti vaimoaan liikaa* (The Man Who Loved his Wife Too Much) 1979, *Kaunis hallitsija* (Beautiful Ruler) 1981, *Vaikka on kesä* (Though it's Summer) 1983, *Teokset 1973-1983* (Collected Poems and Other Pieces 1973-1983) 1985, *Tule takaisin, pikku Sheba* (Come Back, Little Sheba) 1986, *Voiman ääni* (The Sound of Power) 1989.

from **IT'S ME** / MINÄ SE OLEN (1976)

Salome

She'd been round the tracks, changed stables.
    Burnt out, she was:
a black mare, slim and flinching as a flame.
                        Poor Salome...
Bloody horse, Terry – 'the number one jockey' – hissed.
Maybe, I muttered.
    We exercised from time to time,
Salome and I.
  I whistled, sang, coaxed.
    She, she flitted like a bridled bird.
She listened –
        as much as her shyness permitted,
as humbly as her fear allowed.
Something she may have grasped: two oddballs
                        in an odd world,
the dud leading the dud, the sad
catching the blab of the sad.

from **THE MAN WHO LOVED HIS WIFE TOO MUCH** /
MIES JOKA RAKASTI VAIMOAAN LIIKAA (1979)

A Dog Called Julia

Just look at this epitaph with whiskers!
So glad to share my affairs, sometimes
she seems to be bearing my burdens.
A dog called Julia:
half-July half-Yuletide.
Often thought of putting her down, so
she wouldn't need to die.
Smash her skull or break her neck
with my own hands, to stop her mourning
her premature death.

Which seems to go on delaying.
She places her four paws cautiously down, one at a time,
so the Lord won't hear her still about
and whisk her away.
Two years ago, she stepped on some glass, her toe
stuck out, a tendon was cut.
She looked at me. Believe it or not,
I grieved over little Julia's lot:
for a moment I thought the blood
was dripping from my own heart.

Once I nearly got invited to a wedding, one time nearly to a funeral.
And once I was nearly there with the rest
at the chemist's birthday party.
At best, I'm third, fifth or seventh wheel;
sometimes I get a call from a Salvation Army person
who giggles like Marilyn Monroe.
The railway station's an old bat, and every morning it smooths its
wrinkles;
the carriages are in their own place in the siding,
and I'm in mine in the light from the window,
and nothing brushes by the days but
a plaintive wing made out of birds.
There are Pentacostalist invalids here, God's cripple-winged artists;
iniquity shines like moonlight on the bare cheek,
and I'm not qualified for this world's guitar club.
I get my music from frozen puddles in back lanes.
This morning I slopped my *café au lait* down my collar;
I'm scared of death – that way it has
of hanging about all the time.
I move like van Gogh with my ear in my pocket, I listen:
that's harmless there, in the dark grass, is it?
The willow warbler of my mind taps it, thumb-sized,
a ground-nester, a bird of childhood, a raking bird,
with a little clump of grass for nest, exposed
to the world's winds, the rain, the squirrel.
I go with my hair over my eyes, the snow collects on my lids, on my
shoulders.

The town's weird, my heart's weird, the wind whistles and groans,
        old bellows,
the only relief's in sleep:
                        tiredness lets you absorb the night sky.
A cigarette anneals my evenings, a certain reverie, the cigarette's
        burning look,
and beneath the window the fragrance of snow
                                        and an unseen angel.
Weltschmerz – if the word still means anything – I've licked.
I'm never nearly alone, or more or less gone:
if I am, or you're wondering, I'm off.

Once there was a man who loved his wife so much
he'd no strength left for anything else.
His shoes split, his overcoat wore gossamer-thin,
and his shirt buttons flew to high heaven
from the sheer pounding of his passionate heart.
His wife was pushed too far when want pinched,
poverty peeked out of the windows, nothing worked,
and the man did nothing but love.
All this took place in Russia, by oil light,
in the days when people were still rich in snow,
vodka glinted like diamond in its chipped glass,
a slice of cucumber was a gleam in a dream,
and at the corner of the barn by the parsonage
a chime on a dog's lead jingled like dream-sleigh-bells.
One frosty night, it dawns on me:
dogs are the heart's tarts, warm, nourishing,
and somewhere deep in my breast, like a boulder,
there's a fragment of Old Russia, a crumb of crucified love.
The starry nooses are swinging quietly,
the house corner is shrinking and cracking,
something's breaking here in the silence.
Here and there in the snow an old tree's dying:
its wooden heart can't bear such cold.
In the sparkling night God's asleep: it's an old story,
and the moon's got that end-of-the-world look.

from **THOUGH IT'S SUMMER** / VAIKKA ON KESÄ (1983)

Before death itself comes,
it paints the pine boles red
around the house.
It thrusts the moon, the bright moon, into the sky
on edge, like an old dish
whose enamel of light is peeling.
Over this house that night
is now folding over.
And in the changing, embracing currents the house
gets ready, unhurriedly, all by itself
for death.
Long before death arrives
the mountains of the moon rise, set
on this little house that was a home,
that's crouching, breathing scarcely audibly.
The night-hinge turns, the moon goes,
and again returns.
I nail a cross on the door, on the wall,
on the snow and the pine bole,
I light a wax cross
for the stranger to come.
In the night, wave drives after wave,
in the night, the ebb and flow of the snow.
In the night, the pillowslips, the fragrant slips and sheets
swell into sails, into expectation,
navigating from the rib-cage to earth,
to the frosty, resounding earth.
No stop on that road,
no backward look, no
halloos to the frontier.
Let the heart unroll as little red carpets
right up to the gate, let them glow,
carnations against the skin of snow.
You too, little bush, get ready,
licking my window with black flames.
Get ready and be ready.
For death is tender
when it comes.
It hugs you to its breast.
Without a word, it teaches you the meaning of your cradle song,

which it brings you behind your stooped ghost,
behind the years, the decades.
It puts a gift in your infant fingers, a gift
you stare and stare at with dimming eyes.
It gives you the song you thought you'd forgotten.
Its breast and shoulders are garlanded with flowers.
It's hollow, to be able to take in a person completely.
It holds you by the edges.
It spreads you open:
it tries to understand you.
And then it's understood.
It nails your eyes open,
your mouth open, that the
clamour of life is clambering out of.
And you look, not at me now,
through me,
behind me,
at your own death.
And at the white flowers
that have burst out
all round the tiny house.

A brief pale winter day would fit
into the tail-end of a dog.
Like that little life
that fitted so easily
between rowan and rowan.
Winter days are coming, settlers in Snowland,
grief's coming, old acquaintance, signing his name
on the heart's soft skin.
At night the roofs rise and sink –
the sky hauling them in a weird hallelujah.
And through the blizzard I'm awaiting
one thing, one only, a face
whiter than the snow.
I wait, not afraid of anything any more.
I just wait.
But when you do finally come,
years and years from now,
I'll be a crone already, ready to go.
For that's how it is: however long I wait,
here we'll never meet again.

from **COME BACK, LITTLE SHEBA /** TULE TAKAISIN, PIKKU SHEBA (1986)

For me, it's a question of eternity.
But you, you don't love me,
you love your new green jacket,
you sleep with it.
Our cockerel's sleeping with the hat-rack in the hall.
I see you leaving, your back receding,
till you and your coat have disappeared completely:
so often I've done that!
It's a skill I have, a kind of talent;
it can't be acquired,
there's no way in, and if you're in, there's no way out.
But you always come back.
And I watch you and twirl
a raw herring by the tail like an athlete's hammer
and let fly onto the track.
And unerringly it lands by the white
tomcat, the one with the wonky head,
with hurt eyes, spaced out.
Who's got a lesion in the soul,
perhaps some question of eternity.

Come back, little Sheba.
I'm always thinking of you.
My eyes stare fixedly in front,
my face is darkening, evening's darkening into night.
You're a larch among the fir trees in the park,
your relaxed silhouette
wears invisible light.
Like my heart wearing invisible grief.
It's night, moonlight's shadowing the earth,
the trees are silvering over,
and I'm writing this as a prisoner
in the prison of myself.
Your cocked ears are a wild animal's –
they're bound to hear:

Sheba, my heart's calling,
with every beat, ruggedly.
Come back, little Sheba.

I ask what the sculpture's called
and your eyebrows shoot up, astonished:
'Keyhole, of course!'
How can a small almost hollow bit of wood-veneer
with two cockfeathers stuck to it
be called 'Keyhole'?
You pick up a blue stone with a cat painted on it.
Can't I see now: the cat's looking through the keyhole.
Yes, that's it: a window into days and dreams,
into your unfathomable smile.
And into the evening that on the western horizon is
covering itself in gold.

VÄINÖ KIRSTINÄ

BORN 1936

PERTTI NISONEN/TAMMI

Born in Tyrnävä, near Oulu, with dark winters and white summer-nights, the son of a farmer, **Väinö Kirstinä** lives in Tampere and is part of that industrial city's socially concerned ambience: he is abidingly, though with richly varying tones, concerned with the impact of the urban technology and impersonality on human sensitivity.

He has been a news editor, a Finnish-language lecturer and a dramaturge for the radio, but mainly works as a freelance.

A contemporary of Saarikoski, Kirstinä aimed in the sixties to 'break the mould of Finnish modernism – hermetics, for example. I tried to bring everyday language into poetry – trams and fridges alongside the familiar symbols of mountains, lakes, beaches and birds'.

Yet his short oracles and aphorisms, with an oriental brevity and simplicity, suggesting an influence from Anhava, often seem closer to mainstream modernism than he suggests, and at times he has been influenced by surrealism and dada. His cheerful, mocking, anti-academic fables are underlaid by social awareness, irony and anxiety, shifting from politics and pacifism to environmental and ecological concerns; but his poetry has always been ludic, a game with the imagination and words, and his effects seem aesthetic and expressive rather than socially instrumental; and he can be lyrical.

He defends the poet's right to produce without asking why, or where his poetry is going. He traces moment-to-moment perceptions, notating a lonely position in the cosmos. Sharpness of sense-perception, attention to reality, and an eye for the phoney, are tools of 'internal resistance' to the creeping totalitarianism that, he feels, threatens individual liberty and happiness.

He has translated Baudelaire, Breton and Malraux, among others.

POETRY BOOKS: *Lakeus* (The Plain) 1961, *Hitaat auringot* (Slow Suns) 1963, *Puhetta* (Talk) 1963, *Luonnollinen tanssi* (A Natural Dance) 1965, *Pitkän tähtäyksen LSD-suunnitelma* (Long-term LSD-Plan) 1967, *Talo maalla* (House in the Country) 1969, *Säännöstelty eutanasia* (Planned Euthanasia) 1973, *Elämä ilman sijaista* (Life Without a Stand-in) 1977, *Runoja 1958-1977* (Collected Poems 1958-1977) 1979, *Hiljaisuudesta* (Out of Silence) 1984, *Yötä, päivää* (Night, Day) 1986.

from **THE PLAIN** / LAKEUS (1961)

Back home
and crouched over the cottage table
we saw the so-simple grain in the wood
and weariness turned into knowledge:
why we'd gone away
and why we had to:
to come back and see the long home table's
uncharted patterns.

The last night he lay awake before she came
and produced a verbal gem, poor as he was.
How ceremoniously he'd offer it,
how the girl and the gem
would adorn each other.

But morning came,
and they were silent.

from **SLOW SUNS** / HITAAT AURINGOT (1963)

Birds are hullabalooing in the trees –
'Great! Great!' cry the kids.
The rye outside my window is growing
like a great stiff giant.
I go to the window and look out:
the weather's brightening up like a shattered ice-sheet,
and the corn's growing with a crackling noise.
Of all this I'm the father.
I open myself to the floating caresses of the air.

Evening, and an aching red gash in the sky.
Slow slashing shouts cut lesions
in the cattle's frightened silence.
Light beams and sneers.
The continents are growing blades.
Goodly is the kingdom of the dead
the alive are designing.

from **TALK** / PUHETTA (1963)

Breaking

When the forms fade,
people, animals and plants part,
order collapses, it's ebb tide
and divorce is imminent;
you knew enough to expect it all,
unlike the animals.
You're groaning already:
it's hard, it's a grind.
It's only the spot you don't know, the minute:
you might last long or
crack like a pot, a window-pane or a heart.

Encounter

touring the zoo:
a woman with a beautiful shadow

a badger: a humble amble
a tiger: a watching binocular

we said
hello
see you soon

she'd a dog with her
it sat on its bottom
looked at the tiger
peed on a tree
ran to another

from **A NATURAL DANCE** / LUONNOLLINEN TANSSI (1965)

Walker

When you walk out, all the lights burn red and the traffic
gets snarled. The swing of your umbrella keeps time with
the click of your heels. Your eyes are all queen bee and city,
the leaves' edges are smiles in the wind.
The shadows give in coolly to the trees' green.

A seagull flew a pearl of thunder towards the summer
and I heard the last summer and wrote on a cloud's edge;
I curled up my tongue and went silent;
autumn came, nights full of you and bright moon;

it's autumn, bright apples, bright nights, soon
a narcotic scent of snow, mere blue in the black lime tree,
days and nights both full of blue, and now
the green earth giving, silence and throbbing deep in the soil.

from **HOUSE IN THE COUNTRY** / TALO MAALLA (1969)

Rose and Apple

I tucked an old calendar under the rose to make it
    flower at Midsummer, a movable feast.
I buried a wormy bream under the appletree,
    to keep it from the cat.
The rose and the apple have a taste for butcher's bits.
    Give a rose blood and it really blossoms.

from **LIFE WITHOUT A STAND-IN** /
ELÄMÄ ILMAN SIJAISTA (1977)

The quilt has slipped. I cough, swallow some cough mixture and water, smoke half a cigarette. Back to bed. It's spring. I keep clearing the riverbed of slush under the bridge, I'm helping the spring to come. Ice and mud accumulate under the bridge. The piers keep giving, the force of the current smashes the timber supports. Now I'm downstream. A surge is coming. I wade a mile or so downstream in frozen slush, opening the channel. A surge is coming behind me, but it hasn't got to me yet. I'm Kirstinä of the Spring.

They're playing. I wish them luck and hope they get it.

The children's cruel games last till evening.
As Haavikko said, neatly.

If you said it happened every day no one would believe you.

I can't say the right thing at the right time. I write.

I forbade myself the words 'like', 'I' and 'soul'. I sort of
forbade myself poetry.

Nora doesn't go usually. Ibsen was creating theatrical theatre.

Frank speech is indecent, conversation fornication.
Europe's most inhibited people.
Listen occasionally to what they're really saying.

The hot stone that's dropping on your head
from a cloud is always just about to drop.

like children playing on the icy precipice of a rock
and like folk with outlines fading
                                        in a milk of mist
      I inhabit an industrial city
        we ring up in the night sometimes
          we aren't many here

A bulldog bounds about in the shallow snow
jerks its lead in its mouth

    small city, large phone bills
    footfalls die

this city wasn't built for my entertainment
naturally

    'We're just pine needles in this life,
    life wasn't meant for us,'
    says a man on the bus
    on the first day of the year

I try to live my life without a stand-in

like children playing on the icy precipice of a rock
and like folk with outlines fading
                                        in a milk of mist

You've a pencil-stub in your pocket,
a bit of paper
you can quickly stuff away.
You've a lot.

You think the text through
and jot it down.

You end with a short image – like:
    a thistle's flowering by the road,
    dusty, unseen.

from **OUT OF SILENCE** / HILJAISUUDESTA (1984)

A crow settles on the crown usually,
and on the highest pine's crown, that's raised itself
above the others.
When the crown breaks
the tree stops putting out tallness.

Not every tree has the lofty quietus
of a bolt of lightning, as Nietzsche rhapsodised.

'Poets tell too many lies,' he said himself.

branches are hung with silver watch-cases
when a crate of dynamite goes up

the housewife has the dog put down
when the price of food goes up

the cottage roof puts up a nettle
when the tenants have departed

I is a lyrical I
I has an electric typewriter

I is professionally I
I's task is to be I

I gets grants if it's I
but if it's not I it doesn't

What do they say, when all you do is sit and think?
That you're no good as a citizen.

And what-all work are you neglecting, when you sit?
Now you think about it yourself and concentrate.

How many items can you concentrate on all at once?
How many rails can you run on all at once?

empty day, I go for a stroll,
idle, addled,
   aimless, footloose,
not a thing new in sight,
      seen it all before,
and nothing I want to say,
unless death and hell,
      and summer's flowering all around,
red clover, white clover, meadows of buttercups,

   a child bangs her head on a stone, I take her to the doctor
a purchaser offers a considerable reduction on my flat,
I accept

and nothing I want to say

      I come across some wild strawberries, a choice mushroom
   and the clouds

PENTTI SAARIKOSKI

1937-1983

V. NAUMOFF/OTAVA

Along with Haavikko, **Pentti Saarikoski** is the most influential poet in this volume, though vastly different in temperament and fate. Emotional, highly intelligent, imaginative, inventive, rash and unstable, he appealed to the hearts as well as the literary responses of his generation.

Born close to the Russian border, he was exiled to Helsinki with his family by the Russian occupation of Karelia. His last years were spent with his Norwegian wife in Sweden, but facing his early death, he chose to be buried at Valamo, the Greek Orthodox monastery on an island of Lake Ladoga, close to his birthplace.

The son of an office manager, he lived the life of a learned bohemian, surviving vividly in both the contemporary urban world, the Finnish and Swedish countryside and, imaginatively, in the Greek and Roman classics. Saarikoski challenged his own generation not only with his poetry and commitments but his formative translations – Joyce's *Ulysses*, Homer's *Odyssey* and Henry Miller's *Tropic of Cancer*, among others. The colloquial urban Finnish idioms he adapted for *Ulysses* and *The Catcher in the Rye* transformed the literary language, opening up the imaginative potential of Finnish spoken syntax and a judicious use of Helsinki slang.

The language of his own poetry is, however, supple, idiomatic, but classically pure. He writes both short, tightly organised lyrics, and extended sequences that develop an imaginative idea, relating historical and mythological situations to the dilemmas of the individual and society.

His poetry is a record of a disturbed spiritual and intellectual *paideuma* of decreasing optimism. As a young man, iconoclastic, leaning strongly to the left, he mocked all the institutions – church, state, army, the sexual taboos – and was tempted by Marxist politics. But he soon found the totalitarianism of party discipline incompatible with his free-ranging spirit and came under criticism in his turn. The paradoxical mind of a poet, and his desire to destroy the dominant capitalist language, led him into syntheses such as, at the time of the Berlin crisis, 'the walls must be strengthened to make them fall'; or 'the power the system doesn't use is the power that changes the system'. Finally he opted out of organised politics with (loosely translated) 'the socialist dream is not my dream'.

He comes to see himself as a sort of Heraclitus dancing in the eternal flux, with the world as labyrinth and the Minotaur an eternal presence. Hardly a guide, as confused as, if not more confused than, his contemporaries, he is a witness: his success – apart from his outstanding literary gifts – is in charting what it was like to be very much alive, Finnish but unparochial, and seriously preoccupied with a just and enlightened society in a time of world-wide confusion, unenlightenment and injustice.

My Introduction has an extended discussion of this fascinating poet, and Anselm Hollo has published two books of translations of Saarikoski: *Helsinki* (Poetry Europe Series, Rapp & Carroll, London, 1967); and *Poems 1958-1980* (The Toothpaste Press, Iowa, 1983).

POETRY BOOKS: *Runoja* (Poems) 1958, *Toisia runoja* (More Poems) 1958, *Runot ja Hipponaksin runot* (Poems and Poems of Hipponax) 1959, *Maailmasta* (About the World) 1961, *Mitä tapahtuu todella* (What's Going On Really?) 1962, *Runot 1958-62* (Poems 1958-62) 1964, *Kuljen missä kuljen* (I'm Going Where I'm Going) 1965, *Ääneen* (Aloud) 1966, *Laulu laululta pois* (Song Away from Song) 1966, *En soisi sen päättyvän* (I'd Not Let It End) 1968, *Katselen Stalinin pään yli ulos* (I Look Out Over Stalin's Head) 1969, *Onnen aika* (A Fortunate Time) 1971, *Alue* (The District) 1973, *Ja meille jäi kiireetön ilta* (And We Were Left with a Leisurely Evening) 1975, *Tanssilattia vuorella* (The Dance Floor on the Mountain) 1977, *Tähänastiset runot* (The Poems So Far: Collected Poems) 1978, *Tanssiinkutsu* (Invitation to the Dance) 1980, *Hämärän tanssit* (The Obscure Dances) 1983.

from **POEMS** / RUNOJA (1958)

From morning to evening, going leagues and leagues –
the world an insignificant plateau
in you and round you: you're free, all right:
go wherever you like,
you're exceptionally free:
only your speed is decreed.

A wise Greek
called The Obscure
had it right
and now I understand:
I'll never get there by evening
and at night, asleep,
I'll go back to my beginning.

Moving

a big bird needs a big nest
for a little bird a smaller nest will do
wonderful weather you've got for moving
so I have I replied and smiled
dad gave me his hand and said goodbye
mother hugged me and then I left
and the removal van left
easy to lead people by the nose
removal men for instance
I don't as it happens live where the removal man's waiting
and my things are waiting
he can light up yet another cigarette
and it's not my concern
since I'm small and smaller than a little bird

from **MORE POEMS** / TOISIA RUNOJA (1958)

Epigram

Hermes, hey: Maia's son, help!
                    I'm going
finally rigid in this duster.
    Give us a decent ulster
and a drop of wine, if you can.

Hipponax, you got what you asked for,
a coat you're not cold in, and no thirst:
one man's death is another man's epigram.

Old Age

    Oh dear, Dionysus, gaga and doddering!
Down on his knees in the park, hands trembling,
and when his thyrsus snaps, the girls
tumble out of their hidey-holes and twirl away giggling.
    Poor Dionysus!
On his belly in the park, feet north,
beard going green even in death,
and stentorian as a whole city
even in death,
    oh dear, Dionysus.

Varia Hipponactea

1

My wife told me to write no more poems.
Every day I've been buying some American plums –
had visits from the girl with breasts
'so moist and tender you can eat them like candy'.

2

I was faring through the forest to a rendezvous
when my ears pricked up, hovered in the air –
so they said, at least –
to harken a little to the forest sounds.

3

Surrounded by republican beasts he (Kerkidas)
kept his head: he only breathed in.
Zeus made him into a constellation.

4

A tortoise's bath is its own back.
Come rain, it lies back and bathes.

A Marshal of Straw is riding by.
'Where to, Marshal,' the tortoise asks.
'Where to – now I'm old? Keep riding, that's all.'

from **ABOUT THE WORLD** / MAAILMASTA (1961)

I bought a horse from a madman.
He'd sketched it himself
and otherwise it was a perfectly ordinary horse
but its eyes were in its nostrils.
He'd done that
on purpose: so people would see
how mad he was
and buy more briskly.
I bought it.
I thought about the horse: as it would stand in a pine grove
in the evening with blood dripping from the sun's ears.

Potato Thief

The year was as long and dark as a bed,
I slept between two winds;
the bush was filling with black berries.

I went round two museums,
the first for turn-of-the-century middle-class interiors,
the second for state-purchased paintings
suitable for turn-of-the-century middle-class interiors.
The year was long and dark
the forest was pushing through the museums.

In summer the bush bloomed,
I very nearly bought a car
but then I stole a middle-class person's potatoes
and taught them how to behave themselves. Horrible summer!
Autumn gave us the moist glad eye from afar
and I was excluded from all restaurants.

I read some cardboard cut-out poets
with speech coming out of their mouths like writing;
the poets were sitting on wooden stools
in two forests and listening to the moon.

I slept without a pillow in a long and dark bed,
the police set off after me
and the potatoes thumbed their noses at the police.
The suns were small as black berries.
I hopped on a bike and fled from the world.
I pedalled up a hill and a girl was holding a basket,
a girl in a blue skirt, she sat on the bicycle rack.
At the top of the hill I took the girl's skirt off,
the girl opened her basket and tiny lions leapt straight out
and scrambled under the snow to hibernate.

The police were after me.
I leaped off the bicycle saddle through the moon into the sky.
I yelled 'Last one through's a rotten egg'.

from **WHAT'S GOING ON REALLY? /**
MITÄ TAPAHTUU TODELLA? (1962)

I love you
like a foreign country
cliffs and a bridge
like a lonely evening smelling of books
travel the world towards you
under the aerosphere
between two lights
my thought I've carved and you

This began two years before the wars
in a village that now belongs to the Soviet Union
my sole recollection of the war is the fires they were great
they don't come like that nowadays
I run to the window at the wail of the fire engine
I was on the move all my childhood
I turned communist
I went into the cemetery and studied the angels
they don't come like that nowadays –
sella in curuli struma Nonius sedet
I burned books in Alexandria
I played the part of a stone and a flower and built a church
I wrote poems to myself myself the chair went up and down
high-backed ones like that don't come nowadays
high poetry there is I'm expecting a cheque
Which is the mistake, the wrong way, or the right, not the Way
it's ± 2
I live the future times
I read tomorrow's newspapers
I support Khrushchev carry the owl from room to room
I'm looking for the right place for it, This began

I live in Helsinki
Helsinki is the capital of Finland.
It's situated by the sea 120 miles west of Leningrad.
Helsinki is an expanding city, and the rents are high.

We sit in the midst of our forests backs to the giant and watch
 his image in a well. He wears a dark suit a white shirt
and
 a silver tie. In his country everything's different,
 there they walk on their heads or without a head.
We sit in the midst of our own forests,
but far in the West there's a land with coastal waters bobbing
 with big eyes, and they can see this far.
Helsinki's being rebuilt after Alvar Aalto's plan.

I lived in a ruin called The Lion
a woman sat on the floor
her breasts were watching me

Woman a region
a place of birds
with lips down below like willowleaves
L'amor che move il sole e l'altre stelle

I wrote a justified apocalypse
an ungodly play
I was dead
Christ dwindled to a fish
and a flashing eye

a free market economy and the right to say
whatever you happen to say, western countries
I'll chat away the longeurs of this long evening

this evening
            I've nothing special in mind

    the Woman's driven the blatant beast from her thought

if you went on the balcony and had a look
            you never know
    the President's car might be driving
        by you see it sometimes
            in this quarter
    the Finnish lion seesaws a curved scimitar

        now it's like last year
            and two years ago
    a big bottle's been painted with flowers
        the pigeons are clattering in the loft
    you don't notice the building going on

            and his eyebrows
    were like two oriental scimitars
            ready to strike.

            the sun's shining
    a day sunny as a grand hotel and

        it's a floating mine of a star

        a historical procession
            a public demonstration
            shoesoles in blood
                a communiqué

            the tram went
            far beyond the city

        the network of veins
            one gets lost in
        and the windows
            one gets stuck in
                trying to get away

    A car lies on its back in the water

a little cooler
a sky seen as an isosceles triangle with one eye looking out
like an unfrozen spot
an artist strode up St Anne's Street
the bones of the trees stand out now in winter
killing is like letting lots of thin glasses drop

Seek ye first the kingdom of pure practical reason

bits of advertisements and headlines
bits of gramophone records feathers

lighted arches glimmer
and the frontiers are floodlit

when the hour of the snarl-up comes
and the cars crash into each other
and the crack of crumpling metal and people's cries
are heard in the darkness

when the journey is broken, then no one is on the right road

from **I'M GOING WHERE I'M GOING /** KULJEN MISSÄ KULJEN (1965)

Life was a chequered brightness.
The way came from the forest where the pheasants were racketing
at sundown the land was a brilliant green.
Houses meshed with the terrain, the back of my hand smelt warm.
I'd thoughts in my head
which I'll not publish,
as they'd further perverse policies.

I learned new words
such as 'nincompoop' –
meaning what, do you think?
What does an aspen do?
(We've set up house, the train-din is over:)
What other virtues could you find
besides the virtue of ownership?
Everything apparent is substantial, you've a look in your eye.

from **SONG AWAY FROM SONG** / LAULU LAULULTA POIS (1966)

Wonderful is the aura of your eyes
The houses here are rickety the appletrees creak
everything sighs
For one more moment you're close to me then it's
a meaningless whining old woman
The heat of your vagina and the blue mountains
are my peace
I don't remember the journey a bird on the window-sill
and how is death possible
A horse watched us protractedly in a monastery garden
with never a whinny

from **I LOOK OUT OVER STALIN'S HEAD** / KATSELEN STALININ PÄÄN YLI ULOS (1969)

In Helsinki I made a contract for my next book
and thought about socialism.
Popescu was escorted to the station
and after that I went to the market to buy a pike.
I'll cook the pike today.

Socialism's dream is not my dream.
When a woman begins to argue her superior knowledge
she'd better go if she knows where to go.
The elements are polluting.
We won't blow to pieces or melt into stone.
Power's slipping from everyone's hands
and the usurper of power doesn't know
which pie to put his finger in.
But I don't want to hang my opinions out to dry.

My trip to Helsinki's just a blank.
I'm back again.
I put some Insect Oil on Stalin's bust,
he looks dandy with dead flies in his hair.
They say bad things about Stalin –
it's easy about the dead,
but how was he worse than the others?
Had an oven built and pushed the builders in?
What is it I want:
summer, and harebells,
it's terribly cold under the feet.

Must make some nettle soup tomorrow,
it's jolly good because
it has associations:
mother sent me picking nettles
and we made coffee from dandelion roots
when I only had a father now and then.
It's a hard day's night.

Cool
as I walk in the wood, prick in hand,
seeking a pee-place.
Lying this afternoon on my back in pain

I thought of something that ought to scare me:
that everything I've done is black on white;
but it doesn't scare me.
When I came back from my pee, everyone inside was lecturing
with one voice on the theme of virginity,
shouting stereo terzetti on the erotic HI FI,
with the candle drooping, and Stalin's head soberly inclined.
The radio announces news,
then the theme is dreams;
everyone's in a hurry to tell their own,
because it's the best.
It's over now and that bed wasn't my deathbed yet,
though I'd occasion to think so when my heart seized up;
on the other pillow there was an empty hat
and I saw the funny side of it.
Would that straw hat make Tuula laugh?
No: wouldn't have made her laugh,
she'd just have bawled. Oh, how I love her.

from **A FORTUNATE TIME** / ONNEN AIKA (1971)

My thoughts don't change.
They're like carved statues.
I've tried to picture them
the minute they come in view.

Summer's gone
as if everything had.
I sit in a chair or look out,
still walk in the meadow,
but a chill stitches my stomach:
I can't think of anything but my mistakes.

Tender is the hand
that closes the mouth,
tender the arrow that kills:
like a touch of sun.

from **THE DISTRICT** / ALUE (1973)

House and people and trees architect-designed.
From the café window you can see it all.
Soon I'll be as old as I've always been.
I'm beginning to study the history of my characteristics.

But nature's face is calm till the end of the world.
Spring days smell of blurred memories –
a hand, excited breathing.
The forest is an academy the barbarians destroyed.
In the wind you hear
the song of exterminated birds.

I finally wake
to the smell of millions of dandelion-suns,
to a world not in need of your explanations.
A dog's bark: be off.
Don't come here with your shoes.

from **THE DANCE FLOOR ON THE MOUNTAIN /** TANSSILATTIA VUORELLA (1977)

Today I'm going another way
coming to the meadow from the west
I want to see the mountain in unfamiliar marine light

the air is soft paper
on which the trees are blurred signifiers

I'm roaming the meadow
longing to be a poet whose song
would move stones and
organise city walls
make trees walk to carpenters
that build homes for people

An unsubstantial sorrow
is a heavy burden
but still, still I want to see
everything in unfamiliar marine light

[IV]

The serpents with their little tongues
have licked my ears
so I can hear again
the world's rumours
Holy
are the berries on the rowan

I want to keep this peace
with its creatures on my shoulders
its dance floor on the mountain

[V]

The paper tells me 30,000 long-tailed ducks have been shot
and I'm amazed that there's a large population
I've never heard of before
near here, how many other peoples
further off, in the world

I light the oven, sweep the floor
tart up the house for my wife's arrival
go to meet her she's coming by bus
loaded with shopping,
she can carry the validity herself
I'll take the objectivity, it weighs
lighter on me
It's spring already

Last night Nixon wallpapered the walls, today
he's flying to China
the cat's walking the road, the wind's wuthering in the oven
it's not yet dark it's the moment
of labia-black sky

30,000 long-tailed ducks are shot, Russian ducks
Swedish are shot in Norwegian waters
how many peoples further off, in the world

You who think society can be improved
that your and your comrades' works and thoughts
Lenin lies in his mausoleum
so completely dead!
a new clause is being added to the law
prohibiting work against the Law
prohibiting us
and soon nothing will be allowed
except thoughts
that don't know how to die

[VII]

Winter solstice
and the bees cling to each other
in the hive centre
where Jesus is born a honey-scented child

The sun is setting
a scarlet winterball like a fatbellied man
our neighbour, the carpenter
will be rolling into bed

On the first day of the year
I place two white porcelain jugs spout to spout
after thinking all night long
about Marx's mistake

on the tablecloth there are Berghaus projections
the colour
I personally call green

Marx's mistake is Lenin
as Stalin is Lenin's mistake
but Stalin didn't make mistakes

I construct a snowman
a sad fascist in the yard
so some image of this winter will remain
our neighbour the carpenter
bends his knee and takes a snap

A heavy snowfall
should mean a rich harvest

I'll build
a cold church for the fascist
a warm one for Jesus

When with summer's first ill-natured wind
and the guests gone
we come down the mountain
with no protection but each others' limbs
where shall we put our hope?

[XXIV]

On St Stephen's Day
I sit in their kitchen
drink some beer and listen to language
that's their affair, their memories
and I scare: I say something
but it clatters
from mouth to floor like a horseshoe

[XXVI]

When the sun goes down
and the cat has been fed
I light the oven

The sign of the tree is heartrending
now against a coppercold sky

All things visible
are symbols

A shout and a question
are a tree
and a snake:
$

I sit in a chair and toil
as if at a carpet

But three tons a minute
what a gusher!
the gods' power manifesting!
and forcing
study of the omens,
what the birds say

Oil
that sinks to the bottom
unites with the sediment
and reduces the production of edible organisms
with spoilage

that can last
incalculably long

But anyone who intends to go to war
will need oil

I read a book
I take a rest, I walk
the way of the moon

the Godbegotten hero Christ
rises from the dead
and teaches people the art of writing all over again

[XXXI]

Hyacinth month brings warm days,
I sit on the shop steps and watch the air vibrating,
watch the people coming up the hill

After September comes October

Today it was garfish for lunch –
a rare fish in these northern parts

In the hyacinth-and-dandelion time
I feel as if I'd learned to write
songs that follow nature's grammar –
songs I linger in for a while

Hyacinth month brings lambs to the meadow
and lowers the boat in the water
and Galtung predicts the destruction of the West

hands stretch out of the wheelbarrow towards the sky

[XXXV]

from INVITATION TO THE DANCE / TANSSIINKUTSU (1980)

You'll never get to the dance floor
unless your feet are tender enough
to hurry without looking past the snake
without startling it
and over the rowan roots without hurting them

[II]

He was studiedly friendly
for he was a king
who are always fearful

I'd set out to do homage to the new age
and he knew it
so he questioned me seriously
and seriously I lied

And on the sixth day of that January it came to pass
that the bees awoke
and led me
to a high mountain and a church ablaze with candles
and this came to pass so that
the scriptures might be fulfilled

the new age was slumbering on
in its golden cradle
in the sugar bowl
the heirs had mistakenly left on the dead man's table

[I]

No, Quetzalcoatl, don't come back
we adore other gods here now
your feathers are on special offer
in the supermarkets
your lakes are ice
the island-to-island bridges
are exhaust pipes of human distress
from the apartment windows
dud eyes look out
on People's Square
gone red with innocent blood
no don't come back, Quetzalcoatl
stay with the faith of your ancestors

[V]

In Skarhämn
it was lovely today
I sat me down in a caff
the sun was setting
as it always does there
down behind the fish racks
an old man came to my table
thought I was a friend of his youth
and we chatted
comfortably about the life that was gone
slurped coffee
suddenly he was in a hurry
Ingemar would be back
a jet plane scored a sky trail
like an ice crevice
or a wound
a long knife-slash
a chill hit me
I was all alone suddenly
in some kind of terrible funnel
Dubcek had to pose as an ambassador to Ankara
Allende clumsily tried to protect democracy
with an automatic rifle he got as a gift from Fidel
it was waiting for me

the moment of horror
I set off down the street
the kids whooped after me hello
they know me wherever I am in the world
everything was so
keel-upwards
I stood in the harbour and watched the painful
exit of a fishing smack
ice screeching along its sides

[XXVII]

Right till the last
Edvard Gylling was opposed to revolution
said it was bound to end in destruction
but when they were in the thick of it
he joined and
took responsibility

Alone in the Castle Hall at Viipuri
after negotiations with the Whites broke down
he paused a moment by the window
studied the last rags of his troops

soon the snow would be slithering off the roofs
he remembered the birch-avenue on his home estate
in Ikaalinen

the army was massacred

Dr Gylling was regarded
as the worst of the war criminals
because he was privileged by education
he fled to Sweden
slipped disguised through the claws of the Finnish police
in spite of all demands
was not extradited

In Stockholm Gylling worked at politics
till a letter came from Lenin

If Dr Gylling agreed
Lenin would like a word with him
Gylling travelled via Vuoreija and Murmansk to Moscow
and promised Lenin
he'd make a republic of Karelia
it would be quite a job

He wrote in Swedish to his mother in Ikaalinen
So many things in life are changing
but I count myself so happy
that amidst all these changes I have my mother
I'd like so much to ever so little
just a little
stroke my mamma's hand

Gylling worked
the Karelians learned to read
and to thin their forests
it was proposed that Petrograd
should be named Gyllingrad
Gylling said absolutely no
he worked
1935: Finnish-speaking population 142,000
book titles: 610
copies sold: 5,200,000
Gylling was exhausted
his left leg was amputated

When the big purges came
Gylling's closest colleagues began
to be indicted as nationalists
separatists and fascists
Gylling said I'm the organiser of this régime
and I take responsibility
he was switched to Moscow
to research on international economics

They lived in a damp cold hotel room
Edvard and Fanny
Fanny said well I can certainly make this quite comfy
many have it much worse
soon Edvard sat in a train
Fanny was taken away later

on Sakhalin Island Edvard reflected
on Chekhov's book that he loved
where Anton Pavlovich describes the prisoners
chained to their wheelbarrows
their lot to push them
and to sleep with them
no rest for Dr Gylling from his thoughts

[XLVIII]

Tyrants were
people
who undressed
and got dressed
worked into the small dark hours
shuffled papers
and fellow citizens
out of the in-tray
and into the out-tray
now the heart's gone out
of government
the tyrants have been rationalised away
machines that don't tire
don't drink themselves silly
and never shimmy or rumba
are doing the work
they speak like barbed wire
and you can hear what you are
you're one-two-three or four-five-six-seven or zero
these machines would be impossible
if they hadn't been invented

[XXX]

Sir Samuel Baker
in the early 1860s
tried to get Kommoro
the chief of the flatlands

on the White Nile shore
to believe in the soul and its immortality

like water off a duck's back
finally Sir Samuel fell back on St Paul
he took a grain of wheat
dug a tiny hole with his finger in the earth
said when you're dead
you're like this grain of wheat
which I'm now burying
this grain will die
but it will bring forth a plant
in which the form of the original is perfectly preserved

Kommoro said yes
I do understand what you're driving at
but you've got it wrong
when I die I'll rot
as this grain will rot
the plant the grain of wheat produces
is a product
it's a new thing
just as a man and woman's children are
new
previously unknown things

and Sir Samuel wrote
that this wild naked man
hadn't the merest scrap of superstition
he could use
to build
some kind of religious feeling on
their brains were like a flatland bog

[XXXIX]

Human flesh smells bad when it burns
no one's going to roast their fish on that flame
a charring hand jerks out some sort of signal

[LIV]

It was hot in the day
the sun was blazing
the drainpipes began pissing
night was coming

when I climb the mountain
the snowcrust supports me
I have to meet the rowan and the Minotaur
the tree's doing fine
but the monster's looking shrunken
and vulnerable in the bitter frost
he'll have to be fitted with an extra vertebra come summer

I stare down the valley
a kind of river where the snow melted
then froze again
not much for me to look at
the light goes on in Edith's kitchen
she's starting Göran's supper
there are some people I love
but there are also
neatly-dressed precisely-spoken people
whose fingers do piano cadenzas when they eat
The *Encyclopaedia Britannica* in the 1884 edition
points out
that the fontanelle on a negro's skull
closes much earlier than in
other races
cramping the brain
so that it's understandable
how the intellectual power of negroes
resembles that of apes
even more than their physique
a hundred years ago
this is established fact
a hundred years from now
some established facts will look this way
there are all kinds of bipeds
some produce reports
for so-called people's representatives
that so-called voters

have elected in so-called elections
and then these explain
on the television
the left wheezily
the right plummily
that the experts have established that
I went ranting this out
on the mountain
the Minotaur's expression never moved
the rowan moped
as it always does when I open my mouth

[XLIII]

All ye that travail and are heavy laden
you've been swindled
with every recurrent promise of a less laden life
that always piles another bale of straw on your backs
get rich to get the rich off your backs
jabber jabber

I was taxiing home
the kind of day that recalls Heraclitus
sun-blaze on the snow-studded mountain
the world close
as an arm you've leant on before

[VIII]

A bird froze in flight
as if iced in air
then immediately flipped on
no trusting it now

[XIII]

I peer from the near to the far
to Europe's edge and the world's end
The coin I've got is good
but I can't see a corpse whose tongue I could put it under

[XXV]

No postman knocks at the houses of the dead
I sink a hole deep in the soil
put my invitation at the bottom
and top it with juniper twigs
I soak them with aqua vitae
and when the whole thing's flaming
there's such a smoke and stink
the dead rise they have to

they rise behind me on the mountainside
they see my shadow
and they ask me what it is

the world and the world's phenomena
are soon forgotten

[L]

I always seek out a stone
the earth-spasms
and the wind and rain
have formed into a man's seat
a back-support
or where you can ease your elbows on your knees
and run your fingers over the script etched in the stone

[LVII]

from **THE OBSCURE DANCES** / HÄMÄRÄN TANSSIT (1983)

a girl
dandy as a dandelion
took me by the hand and said
I'm the light that will lead you into darkness
No crop to brag about when I dig the potatoes
summer was dry, I was lazy
dandy as a dandelion
We have to sleep half on top of each other
legs curled up
these beds aren't meant for people our size
I natter with the magpies about how all
the world's people
are my children and you're the light
dandy as a dandelion who will lead
me into darkness
I've eaten of the knowledge of good and evil
the heavens are clouded
the philosophies and policies crack like dry twigs

a dog or, on a closer look,
an Egyptian princess
with two servants
came to greet me
I couldn't interest her in anything
I showed her a jackstraw board, an English jackstraw board
it's a black disc and from the centre
yellow rays fan out
the rays can't leave the circle, I said, and demonstrated
here in the North, I explained,
the sun is hung
on a branch for the winter
My father's power is greater than the sun
the princess said
don't found any clubs or corporations

I'm the Way I walk along
a delegation, a theory, painfully
since I'm an old and acclaimed man
chosen for this task
to plod up the mountain, to a pedestal
to see the world from
the cornfields, the ocean,
people at their labours, a working man
turning a concrete mixer, a farmer
studying his ploughlands, and in the post office
the post being sorted and in the cemetery
the crosses rotting
I've come to the mountaintop to say my goodbyes
to poetry, here they are, the carved statues
no more need to mention their names
they wrote books, founded religions, ordered
their embalming and they were embalmed
There were no blackberries at first this year
then a few came
tiny ones that when it did finally rain got waterlogged
I sat on a stone, the stone I'm sitting on
I reflected
This world's a universal cemetery,
a goodbye and finally
it's me leaving and no one saying goodbye
propping a cross on my grave to rot
it's getting dark and the days
are uncoupling like foul-smelling railway carriages
No longer governed by the sun
they're creating an art
that all the churches
curse , I've seen
that gesture and can never forget it

You ask me what I am
I'm everything
I know
you ask me just as I'm setting out
how long I'm going to be away
I'll be away until I'm here again

You're badgering me with your silly questions
quizzing me
when I'm setting out to know
what now I don't know

The Obscure is dancing
alone, the trees don't talk to him
the bird
doesn't look
the bear's gone to his lair
to sleep, not a thought about waking up now
The Obscure is dancing
he's forgotten
not only what happened but his memory too
studies spiders,
the cobweb
is the spider's face and fingerprint
The trees have something else to do, get rid of their leaves
The Obscure is dancing
he was involved in government, went into it deeply
studied the psyches of his subordinates
and their behaviour patterns
The spider's web is individualised, decomposes in the evening
the spider can't repair it doesn't die
The Obscure is dancing
in his official state-duties he had managed
to verify that his colleagues based their conception
of state
administration
partly on wishful thinking regarding
their own resources
partly on the neighbouring government leaders'
economic inexperience
The bird's not looking, the bushes
stiffen into stalactites, the spider
doesn't die, its web just decomposes, the dew
in the morning fluffs the filaments like hair
The Obscure is dancing
he thought

that the sun was
new every morning
like the spider's web
He thought the bear's sleep was the bear's work and he thought
sleep the universal ground
he entered a cool grove
where the thinkers gathered
drinking wine and talking
The Obscure dances, the bear sleeps
soon the spider will spin his web again
His theory didn't strike the thinkers as interesting.

It's beginning to blow, I'm homeward bound
from mushrooming,
some choice ones in my basket
The bits of grit make long shadows on the road
though it's only mid-day
I cast a proud eye on my mushrooms
If I didn't know I lived in that house I'd think
happy people were living there
my handwriting wrinkles and shrinks, writing is my skin
Back home I get a mushroom casserole going
even last year, I remember
in and around the house there were still so many people
that now when there's nobody
it seems cramped
the potatoes are simmering
They weren't living people
dead long since, that I chatted with
and death didn't part them from me
life parted me from them

I was poking about in the junipers and the drystone wall
for a schnapps bottle I'd hidden somewhere
The Girl appeared, licked her ice, turned up her nose and said
you're daft
you're for ever seeking the way
down the mountain and out of the wood
and out of your obscurity
you shout

for your dead friends
that you long for
as a bald man longs for his hair, don't you understand this
The girl licked her ice superciliously
you don't understand
in the obscure
the reddest red
the red of a red frostbitten lingonberry looks black
that's what's happened to your friends
I'm the light
that will lead you into darkness

I'm not talking about the world and its places
but about places and their world
what I'm saying can't be refuted
I started to teach the magpies table manners
they got the point immediately
that now they had to eat their food
each standing on his own stool
no hopping on the table, there were many dissidents
you always get some of them in any benevolent régime
I reflected,
supposing I was appointed the task
of forming a government, would I choose my ministers
from those who hop on the table
or from the others who stand on
the stools intended
for round a foot-high flat stone on the lawn I've put
six foot-high stumps
as stools for the magpies
so they can learn table manners
The magpies fly down for their breakfast as soon as they spot
me at the kitchen table
eating my own and
reflecting, night's not a problem, it's days
night doesn't press on you but the days
would be unbearable if the magpies rejected me.

the swans begin
to gather
in the bay, like members of parliament

circulate asking the latest news, look carefully
to see what the form is
I make the sort of observations a melancholy person makes
the boat's been left
rotting in the water
now the one who sat in it and rowed it
is dead
he died unexpectedly, it was expected
as his style of life was not
healthy, swans
are mean birds, bad birds
they run over the water behind the islands
I've got to take the return journey, I reflect that when
a man
when he is
dead
he should be put in his boat which is a woman
it's his woman
into his carefully-tarred boat and burnt
towards evening so that through the smoke the sun
will shine on those he was dear to
a man's boat mustn't be left to rot
Must sit down on these beachhouse steps a moment

I thought about the leaves on the tree
and the twigs they're fastened to, I thought about looks
that reify me,
make me
a commodity
I ought to lie down
for this work of studying the world, and not myself
but when the world's a big eye that scrutinises me
a censorious eye, a disobliging cunt
On the table I've a lobster
that's reaching with its feelers as if to say something
for it might have a lot
to say about this table and the milieu otherwise
it's been escorted to, wooden forks
and spoons and scoops in a bowl that was glazed
with the use of salt, it has bluish images, I'll go and
scrutinise them closer

the tide was high, the sea blackish
the waves steepening from shore to open water
the wind bit your neck, our deeds
our thoughts and desires
are left as facial expressions, it's difficult
to decide in advance, to explain afterwards
I looked at a house on a hill-shelf, recalled the war years
some end-of-summer evening on the green fellside
when the grown-ups
were dining on crayfish and clinking
I've never seen
any life in this house
though the way certainly goes up there
it's not derelict, just unoccupied
I'm too thin to fill out my jacket
The water splashes over the stone steps
fish with little legs are scrambling along the bottom
then night comes
night with its long fingernails, the holy dark
to load the boat
I push it into the water
not knowing
where the sea will take it or who will unload the freight

on the longest night of the year
it's a starlight night
the girl is sitting on the kitchen sink and singing
the mice are constructing their corridors
He decides to kill the girl as he's scared of death
he helps her on with her coat
puts a sheath knife in his pocket
they leave for the mountain
the blackberries are frosted with hoar and the girl says
you left them unpicked
they climb the mountain, the Minotaur's asleep, the girl says
he takes her by the hand
they walk down Theory Thoroughfare
reach the dustbin
and see the stars again, the pieces of sky

PENTTI SAARITSA

BORN 1941

IRMELI JUNG / WSOY

Pentti Saaritsa's father, a plumber by trade, was killed in the war. Saaritsa, born in Helsinki and educated there, still works in Helsinki as a freelance and translator. He taught Latin-American literature at both Helsinki and Turku universities, and he has translated a great deal from Spanish. He has been a cultural editor for a leftish newspaper.

In his youth he was moved by the politics of Chile and Cuba, but his approach to his art is conservative in the best sense: poetry involves an acute responsiveness to associations of word, image and concept; and the poet is one who observes surprising connections. He is by nature defamiliarised and a defamiliariser. A poem is a telegram from the deeper mind, with news that would otherwise be undelivered. The insight, the grasp, the hit ought to be sudden. Nevertheless the items belong in a large and developing whole.

Saaritsa's poems celebrate, explore and respond uneasily to the spiritually haunted material world. He accepts a materialistic metaphysic and the limitations that implies, while remaining open to intuitions of the mystery of the material. His poems lean to eros and thanatos, to the sensitively sensual, while retaining their social and urban awareness.

In the world, the news is always awkward. Saaritsa will never find belief easy, knows he will never know, but will never agree to be silent. In his 'two-legged house', slightly scared like the children, he listens as the new room is being prepared, even though there are so many rooms already.

He is fascinated by music, and there are constant informed references to it in his work. Each step he takes is an augmented fourth, a tritone, that difficult interval known as 'the devil in music'. He is also working on a libretto.

POETRY BOOKS: *Pakenevat merkit* (Fugitive Signs) 1965, *Huomenna muistan paremmin* (Tomorrow I'll Remember Better) 1966, *Varmuus kerrallaan* (Certainty at a Stroke) 1967, *En osaa seisahtaa* (I Can't Stop) 1969, *Jäsenkirjan lisälehdet* (Additions to the Membership Book) 1971, *Syksyn runot* (Autumn's Poems) 1973, *Tritonus* (Tritone) 1976, *Yhdeksäs aalto* (The Ninth Wave) 1977, *Nautinnon suola* (Savour's Salt) 1978, *Mitä näenkään* (What I See) 1979, *Ovi ja tie* (The Door and the Road) 1981, *Takaisin lentoon* (Airborne Again) 1982, *Runoja 1956-1982* (Collected Poems 1956-1982) 1983, *Taivaan ja maan ero* (The Difference Between the Earth and the Sky) 1985, *Maailmaa köyhempi* (A World Poorer) 1988.

from **FUGITIVE SIGNS** / PAKENEVAT MERKIT (1965)

Rain Psalm

Rain on the way, tall and stalwart: everyway a big blond person.

Bent a little forward, its step is short, no face as yet, but palms warm and broad.

Hardly anything has less choice: always moving towards upturned eyes.

Intending to topple on the landscape's doorstep, it does: it flops down flat on its just-forming face.

The whole landscape is its death mask.

All the puddles are its eyes: blue and brown. For the first time it sees: the sky.

from **CERTAINTY AT A STROKE** / VARMUUS KERRALLAAN (1967)

Face

She was so near she was more smelt than seen and
so distant eye didn't sustain her eye
Who would believe as yet
she meant to change so much
In the rose of dawn her eyes deepened and began to endure
the first small features began to form round them
And underneath a lamp went on and off
as her clothes went off and on

Until her traits continued into her shoulders, her breasts
and her belly and the conversation fairly shared itself
wherever there was skin enough
A new mouth breathed from her hands and groin
and little motions of warmth smiled
from a fulfilled whole face

from **ADDITIONS TO THE MEMBERSHIP BOOK /**
JÄSENKIRJAN LISÄLEHDET (1971)

Hommage au Travail des Chiens

In this park dogs are strictly forbidden
but an alsatian's crouching in the hard snow to shit.
Tail along the ground, like the bottom bough of a spruce,
he's following with his eyes
the industrious municipal tractor
as it impends along the path
    with a fresh douche of snow in its loader.

Now the tractor's passing him, a yard off,
the alsatian turns into a snowdog
but he doesn't pause in his business.
That's how clever he is.

from **TRITONE** / TRITONUS (1976)

Windhoned cantilevers of snow in the couloirs of black rooves.

On my desk an open Pantovski: 'After Meštšera I began to write in a completely new way…'

Half a year, and I've achieved nothing. I'm tangled up in the curtains I'm trying to draw aside from a large window.

My cupboards are stuffed with silent instruments, the loveliest music in the world.

La Valse's vision: blue lapping of restless water that a violin neck suddenly rises from.

A violin silence is always provisional.

A blackbird flitted to the park tree as if bidden.

The news is bad.

I can never believe.

I shall never know.

I'll never agree to be silent.

I see.

Out of the bowels of each block
it comes – that one unidentifiable sound.

Sometimes like a drily dripping water, sometimes
as if a stone were biting a crumb out of itself.
Or a child awake in the dark were learning the word 'hair'.

And the flat-dweller notes it, enters it perhaps
as a comma in the interrupted treatise of his consciousness
when it makes him nervous.

What – again so soon – is it coming from me
or some dead structure?
An alarm. Has anyone else heard it?

No use pressing your ear to the radiator –
the sound never comes from where you listen
but from the dim stairway of listening itself,
those banisters of vacillation and doubt
and the forebodings of new buildings rising behind them.

If the name of the piece is 'Nightpiece',
construct night round it
or there'll be no night.
If the title of the poem is 'Son of the Sun',
it must be yours, everyone's
that reads it.
Through your tears
the smiling girl in the drawing smiles more clearly.
And you'd not evade a single misery or ecstasy
even if you never read, saw or heard a thing.
Everything's there within you:
love and the art that comes from its absence,
sense and the mad world made from its absence.
Whoever you are, choose yourself, always unknown in advance,
make yourself, try to have time.
Keep asking and going. Night will come without fail,
always: driving up with knowledge.

I saw a play
at the children's theatre.
In my lap, a four-year-old:
how his head swung
as the action strode
across the stage!
I sat with the theatre
in my lap.

So many, so many tones,
so many rooms
in the two-legged house.

Someone inside me sometimes rises, opens the door,
is about to go, fading his painful tone away.
Like the eight-year-old today who accidentally
dislocated his friend's arm
and then cried with all the class watching.

I've not let him go, not him either.
I'm in need of all the voices. The whole chord.
It's not yet complete.

A new room's in progress. I sit in its centre,
in a wicker chair, my ear pricked.

From the previous tone to this is a tritone: on a distant
French horn against a storm-tossed forest of strings.
I'm changing so much
my house shakes.

The children in it are listening, prematurely aged,
and a tiny bit scared.

The flesh makes shapes,
grows distant scapes from the head down,
misty forests of hair, remote
wrinkled nests
the hand seeks, the fingers
grope for in sleep.
It's a world, ear and armpit.
The belly.
A wind of reminiscence goes over the slopes of the coccyx,
some strange hand like
your own in its coming.
In the brain a sea moils
and from moment to moment
the capillaries like a name for something merely non-existent
work on and on.
The flesh creates its horizon, awaits
its strange rosy dawn
in every night of the world
and in the forest of the sheets pulsating greetings
murmur from the human engine room.

from **THE NINTH WAVE** / YHDEKSÄS AALTO (1977)

Again I hear that hawking in my skull –
the throat-clearing death opens the dialogue with
in my decades-long quango, this soporific think-tank.
I won't take part, it's evening,
a sky snoozing to rosiness over the street,
and a moment when life
aspires to appear so completely one
you could shroud it with a single poignant feeling
and write it off at a stroke.

from **SAVOUR'S SALT** / NAUTINNON SUOLA (1978)

Message

All this summer night
I've been translating, and now that the universe
has made the lamplight invisible
and the work has seasoned awareness, an eye opens
on a greenish horizon, childhood,
who stares trustingly
over the tangled thickets of youth
at this desk-hunched dawn-watcher,
a stare that brushes his temple, settles on his eyes
that continue the same stare,
and suddenly targets a more elderly figure
on the paper's snow,
a backwards-glancing man near a roadbend.
He plods on never stopping
and disappears.
No trace of a soul.
And everpresent as the blood.

from **THE DOOR AND THE ROAD** / OVI JA TIE (1981)

Vision IV

Street sunlight cut
by sheet-metal cutters of shadow
in a select suburb of ancient
absurdly dilapidated peace

when round the corner darts –
Wagner, no:
a Wagnerian spectre, darting from light to shade.

I see the sun slicing
both of us, my sleep-bedevilled eyes
and, haring across the street, a smirking
knickerbockered-sidewhiskered-kneestockinged man –
and I *know*
the only thing that separates us:
I see him but not he me:
I'm alive.

from **AIRBORNE AGAIN** / TAKAISIN LENTOON (1982)

For Pertti Nieminen at
Porvoo Lyceum, 12.5.1982

A sage old man,
like that crystal chandelier in failing light,
when you don't quite know –
is it still lit by the sun's glow
or itself alight?

from **THE DIFFERENCE BETWEEN THE EARTH AND THE SKY / TAIVAAN JA MAAN ERO (1985)**

The difference of each from each:
the wall from the wind, the wind from the hair
and the hair from the caressing hand –
one silence from another –
like earth from sky – and
the puddle from its mirroring eye.

The first wings
almost find themselves
like a wild strawberry or a four-leaf clover.
They provide childhood's long glide
and fretful forgetfulness.

The next wings
you yourself must string together
from a world of broken splinters,
your own and other people's. Staying in the sky
means grimacing, grinding and
having faith, godlessly, in your lie.

The third wings
hatch under the others,
with hot handholds and smouldering edges.
Blow by blow they fan the fire,
burn and swish and roast like hell.
You can fly with *them* as well.

EIRA STENBERG

BORN 1943

PERTTI NISONEN/TAMMI

The daughter of a Tampere accountant, **Eira Stenberg** studied piano at the Sibelius Academy, noted for its demanding entry, and is now a freelance in Helsinki.

In contrast to some of the other women in this volume, Stenberg has no hypnotic sensibility in her work. Dream imagery appears, but she is wide awake. Whatever the antonym of sentimentality is, she has it.

The ruthless conflicts of marriage, divorce, motherhood and childhood are given a ruthless eye – and seen as the origins of other forms of ruthlessness: 'The concentration camps are set up at home.' Her politics are largely family politics but point towards the larger world of hatred and alienation.

Is her probing of the sinister practices of love therapeutic or itself a form of hostility? In the protectively constrictive ruin of homelife, the male certainly meets a hostile, uncharmed feminist eye, levelled like a rifle muzzle; but the mother too comes under its gaze, as does the rather demonic child. Yet there is evidence of concern, too, and warnings. Her bias shows signs of wounds, and she evidently would like to prevent, if she can, the infliction of more wounds in the next generation. She wants to clear the air, for under the smokescreen of innocence 'The barbed wire cuddles round us / and blooms with roses.'

This might suggest nightmare confrontation, but the tone is playful, and she writes with excitement, wit and zest. She gives pleasure, and one intuits a balance of positive care and concern in her inspiration.

She has also written many children's stories and is now carrying on her war in her novels.

POETRY BOOKS: *Kapina huoneessa* (Revolt in the Room) 1966, *Rakkauden pasifismit* (Love's Pacifisms) 1967, *Vedenalainen silta* (The Submerged Bridge) 1979, *Erokirja* (Book of Resignation) 1980, *Parrakas madonna* (Bearded Madonna) 1983.

from **BEARDED MADONNA** / PARRAKAS MADONNA (1983)

The Eighth Day of the Week

1

It's hotter today than skin, a hundred in the shade.
I'm mixed up in a crime.
It's my task to find out who the murderer is
that's holding the family in terror.

She's a way of striking secretly,
kills child after child.
She has a sign
that shows her presence:
a pile of twigs appears on the oven,
and the next one knows
her turn has come.

When all the other children have been killed
and I alone am left,
I suddenly see the sign, the twigs.

Mummy's coming towards me,
feeling affectionate,
wanting to cuddle me in her lap
and promising protection.
I give her a look
and say I know
who the murderer is
and she won't succeed with me.

2

Good hidings enough
to make a birch-broom:
I chuck the twigs in the oven –
no love no hatred burns
like your presents of them in childhood.
Those souls in the cots,
they're flickering blue flames,
marsh lights in dim fens.
Only the heart can burn like that, smouldering on
without turning to ash.

The world reeks: the concentration camps
are set up at home.
Sooty, those slap-marks on the cheeks.
The barbed wire cuddles round us
and blooms with roses.

4

The heat's getting more and more stifling.
The oven's glowing bright red!
The mothers' haloes are blazing –
better not touch them.
The porridge is boiling over,
bubbling and simmering the kitchen full,
inching upstairs to the nurseries,
into the cots
where the quilts are imperceptibly mutating
into soil.
Suddenly in the yard the birch-whip tree
bursts into flames
the air boils like water
and the sky rains frenzied birds.
A child comes thrusting out of the fire-grate,
laughing as it's born.
Only prophets laugh as they're born –
they know childhood's the worst betrayal.
She's decided to give it the slip.
Quick as a flash, she's milked her mother dry
and grown up. She can't cry.
For her everyone's heart is a fuse.
She runs out
into the street
and kicks to death
the first old lady.

7

No one can detect if a child's dead
provided it's been filled with porridge.
The cleverer the child,
the more obedient,
so that anyone you like can see
how well-bred she is.

But you mustn't forget the lucky coin and some treacle,
or when she's big she'll claim
there's something missing –
like the stuff of life.

Even though she if anyone
should feel stuffed.

Little Criminals

To begin with they're sweet:
they grow tiny nails and teeth.
Who'd guess they'd turn
into sabre-toothed tigers?

When she'd learned how to kiss,
out of sheerest love
she gobbled her nurse,
gnawed the bones clean
and finished as full-up as a dug grave.

A liar sat in a buggy.

A black horse was hitched to the front of the waggon.
They put a child next to him and the horse turned white.

They put another and the horse sprouted wings.

She was a naughty girl: I couldn't play with her.
She nibbled her finger, drew filthy pictures.
I was on my own.
We met in a dream in a strange house:
a woman approached me
in a pale yellow dress,
glimmering like a primrose under trees.

I didn't recognise her but did the fear.
Before I could get away she grabbed my elbow.
Wearily, as if she'd had enough, she said:
'What your philosophy amounts to is me.'

Bearded Madonna

In Santa Sophia at Ohrid
a Madonna has been painted with a beard.
My knowledgeable Macedonian friend explains:

'The artist, so he thought,
was supposed to paint a Christ –
and then forgot to wipe the Mother's beard.'

I do prize people's wisdom:
no one has annihilated
a child's daydream.

A giant bites off the sky:
soon no twinklings
but the village lights on the mountainside
like his gold fillings.
The darkness could make you take them for stars.

Over all there's a milky breast of moon.
There's a sob of water, like pantings in a park,
a scuffle on a bench
when the folds of a dress are thrust back.

The river's lapping the bridge piers,
an astounded cat flashes between the trees,
and for a moment a black queen
sits on a bench with her hat askew.

We're all unsettled, the sky's black.
The stars have been picked and put in the shop windows.
Gold and silver are glittering.

Santa Claus scarlet in crinkly paper
asks outside a department store
if the child has been good.

The child sees it's really a balloon-seller
with human heads bobbing on strings
and bursts into tears.

Money doesn't stink, it's lack of money:
stinks of pea soup, herring, sausage,
depression as the days draw in.
The letter-slot spits bills on the floor.
Morning dawns with weariness
and the loom of work.
The only adventures come in dreams:
the heroic trails peter out
as dawn points.

The newspaper's obese
and half of it's horror
half flash.
It's a bloodstained packet of pictures
of Santa Claus.
Hold it carefully
or a stack of guns might clatter onto the floor.

Spring Storm, the Milky Way

Sturm und drang. Our street's got the spring!
Braids of brook explode into ponds,
water and snot flow
sap's rising in the dogshit-composted trees
and the children are digging sandcastles
out of the sludge – the Park's only Atlantis.

Sooty light streams from the windows
ripples up the slush on the outside steps
where the kids are wheedling April with wet mittens.

A storm's brewing, it bangs open the outside door
and a pike peeks across the lintel.
A bogey socks in the radiators
and the neighbour's cactus on her staircase
bursts into bloom
dragging a crimson robe across its thorns.

The blackbirds are colonising the trees
and in the pissing-down park
wave after wave of lime trees are cresting like breakers.

The car parked by the pavement
looks like an amputated dog's head.

And when the storm's passed,
Knowledge comes, crowning you with nettles.
'Poet,' she whispers,
'life's a boat on fire,
an anchor, a king's rusty crown,
and in the muddy wombs of queens
vacant navel strings are dangling.'

And in May, in the morning,
we sailed over the sea's
subsided towers,
temptation's swinging cradle,
the suddenly offered beds,
wounded childhood's lost home,
salvation through salt.

We passed over them
as if passing understanding.

My child, my mourning dress,
shadow-eyed house,
I'm a crossroads where innumerable paths
twist and turn towards you.

    Like a cuttlefish
    I conceal myself
    so you can't find me.

    Listen,
    mothers live in a gingerbread house
    and stir a witches' brew.

    Mothers charm their children
    into visions of love's blinding flowers.

You flutter in the warm garden
like a serious glance
till it's evening and the lights go on.

Then you're a house, a ship with lights,
    and oh how I'm terrified
    someone in the garden will tumble on a scythe.

Up from the depths I've thrust you
into the ranks of the dying.
    And now, my five-year-old,
    I'm terrified of your grief
    when you demand the impossible:
    that I'll never die.

If I were good at deceiving, I'd think up
diamonds with battleships inside.
If I were the moon, I'd lift
the sea up and look at the ocean floor.
If I were the sea, I'd freeze
a glass lid over the top of me for ever.

RISTO AHTI

BORN 1943

ERKKI KUKKONEN/WSOY

Risto Ahti offers the sole example of prose poetry in the book – an unfashionable form in England; yet Ahti is surely interesting enough to overcome any reader's prejudice against the form. His highly individualised images and landscapes, surreal only in manner, make their own sense, conveying an intense and obsessive curiosity about people, the world and the erotic.

This is a new invention of an ancient way of seeing, something like a personal and sensuous version of Vedanta: we are deceived by words and ideas; reality is waiting to be explored, if we are willing to get lost in it. Valuable experience, including authentic passion, begins when we break the taboos and walk through the fearful warnings of conventional thought. This way knowledge as experience begins, and the problem of knowledge is particularly acute in love.

Importantly, from the point of view of poetry, he has managed to concretise his vision in striking stories and images, with precise outlines, and without the abstract and sometimes vapid philosophising this style of approach can lead to. He has been helped in this by the example of Haavikko and Saarikoski. Adapting their aphoristic and surrealistic narrative manner for his own distinct and completely individualised purposes, his metaphysical stance is distinctly at variance with their defeated pessimism.

He does have a tendency to the didactic, which is best controlled: we might occasionally feel got at. But his intelligence, urgency for understanding, constant sense of much at stake behind the dandified surface, and his constantly shifting boundaries, keep the reader on the alert and searching for meanings.

He is the son of an engineer, was born in the industrial city of Lahti and lives in Tampere, Finland's largest industrial town, with its very vigorous and distinct cultural drive; but this industrial background and its social bias are not emphasised in his work. He has, however, conducted influential creative writing courses in Tampere. In 1987 he took part in the Iowa International Writers' Programme.

POETRY BOOKS: *Talvi on harha* (Winter is an Illusion) 1967, *Runoja* (Poems) 1968, *Unilaulu* (Dream Song) 1972, *Katson silmiin lasta* (I Look the Child in the Eye) 1974, *Oli kerran kultakettu* (Once there was a Golden Fox) 1975, *On myös unia* (There is Sleep Too) 1977, *Aurinkotanssi* (Sun Dance) 1978, *Lintujen planeetta* (Planet of Birds) 1979, *Ja niin rakentuu jokin silta* (And That's the Way a Bridge is Built) 1981, *Narkissos talvella* (Narcissus in Winter) 1982, *Loistava yksinäisyys* (Shining Solitude) 1984, *Läsnäolon ikävä* (A Longing for Presence) 1987, *Laki* (The Law) 1989.

from **NARCISSUS IN WINTER** / NARKISSOS TALVELLA (1982)

Porcelain Girl

Even though she's dressed in long pale dragging garments, she looks naked.

Her skin's extremely white. She's a china doll that's never been painted.

Life eludes her, so I know she's concentrating on death as hard as I'm concentrating on her.

With my fears, I feel aged and angered, but I daren't touch her. I daren't! I dread her skin really might be…wax? china? Perhaps the heat of my passion wouldn't be enough to resurrect her? Her alienation might clang coldly on my soul like a bell-clapper.

If I did impregnate this moon-Diana, she'd give birth to things: bones, snow, guns, curdling music, a colonel, a diamond sword

Poppy

You dress madly: gold, silver, purple – I blush for you in the street, because you're lovely as a flower and live as if life were nothing but wedding rites. And yet your dress says, 'Danger. Poison.' And you force me to think of the cowards who can only see your amorality – not how you fulfil the lust for life.

What is it that makes me glory in the midst of man's grey forest? This: even though you deck yourself as a queen the wise long to shower with all their property, merely to get a drop of life in their veins, you take your clothes off for me and, drawing me down to cover your nakedness, say 'Now I'm in my robes!'

Shame as a Source of Energy

I admit it, I love many, everyone, when I'm loving you alone. As night and day meet, nature goes completely quiet; even the wind goes dumb at this frontier.

The morning light strikes, how wildly and bewilderingly, into you!

It was always very quiet when we met. I loved it most when inner pressure twisted our mouths dumb. All at once we were being without being: nature roared around us, heaps of stones turned into mountains, the flowers reached for the clouds, the grass was high as the roof.

In the Morning

I observe you sleeping: sharp fingernails, bare shoulders, your nape. I hear your faint moan. In the morning you tell me, 'I was going across a snowy plain; someone, far off, was weeping.'

Sometimes you're really beautiful – like an abandoned house's broken window, that the wind goes through without knowing anyone.

You rise and wake. I see the wind has torn its shoulder on the window's jagged edge.

The Clock Lurks on the Wall

The clock lurks on the wall. It looks on – a cold, toothless moon. It lurks and wastes my time. It's a thief, it diffuses warmth, conveys cold.

Darling! More than the clock of your face, I desire the hour-glass of your body.

This bodily clock depends on our desire. It makes me think warmly of previous generations who measured time with the movements of their hands.

The One Whose Words are the Weightiest is Right

The girl was forced to bend to the floor, and a huge stone was lowered on her head. In this way she learned to know the truth.

All one, to the truth, whether she suffered wrong or not.

Only oblivion can wipe away the taste of shame from a burnt mouth.

I insinuate my way through the mass of facts like a snake – so cunningly and nimbly, I'm like an immovable stone.

'What a cynical approach!' you tell me. I smile cynically: 'Make me believe you want answers to your questions. If the scent of a flower deceives a bee it may be genuine.'

There are Poisons that Work so Quickly You Haven't Time to Say Thanks for the Meal

He came and said, 'Eat somewhere else – not from this tree.'

Mentally I saw him walking in the garden and thrusting thorns in the fruit. A moon rose – enormous, silver; the earth slipped by it like a cloud. I asked, 'Did you create me a man or a child?'

What I see is: a snake billowing on the earth, spiralling like a wave in the wind, and in the woman there burns some flame, unidentifiable, hotter than the sun.

A Rite

A scientist is driving in a custom-built car hot after imaginings that contain the cornerstones of his personality.

His physical rapture keeps on asking, 'To whom, to what could I abandon myself utterly?' The sun's pullulating in his long spindly limbs.

In his room, a poet is mourning the lost light of melodies and images. Everywhere we witness dying soldiers.

Who are the barbarians – the priests and judges? The barbarians violate reality with their names, questions and options. They consider them possibilities, and in realising the possibilities create chaos.

Hand me the Philosophers' Stone. I want to smash the neighbour's living-room window.

Happening

I don't claim that nothing happens. When a bird flies back and forth, its nest is forming, or a chick's growing.

Waves do flow to the shore, and further out a boat is going somewhere. I know the return's already planned. I wait, and I see the boat's lights in the autumn evening.

What I think is: we describe circles round ourselves, without going anywhere. I think this once more at the station, when the woman asks, 'Return?' Unaware, I say aloud, 'In reality, though, you can never go back,'

My voice is so odd, the woman looks up and stares at me; she checks softly, 'So – it's just one way?' Agh! It's a tourist's world.

In the train, like a bird flying back and forth, or a boat whose owner has already planned its return, I bump into an unknown person. I fly against a wall, I steer onto a rock.

from **SHINING SOLITUDE** / LOISTAVA YKSINÄISYYS (1984)

Ramblers are Dying Out

Encountering a depressed man, a woman asked him to look at the sole of his foot. There was a thorn in it. As the woman knew life, she asked him, 'Is this thorn essential? Do you love affliction?'

Valleys can't teach you mountain experience, however much you deepen them. Valleys do deepen: and mountains can be suddenly undermined. But so long as they exist, you can climb them and observe the valleys' breadth and beauty.

The woman who knew life said, 'Ramblers are dying out.'
And added, 'There's good reason for rambling – at least enough to make a thorn begin to avoid your foot.'

In the Middle of the Forest there's a Wonderful Garden the Children Remember

When a child wants to go in the forest, father says (he's really sure), 'The forests are full of wolves. The wolves howl like this – and eat up little children. So don't go in the forest.'

When the child anyway decides to go in the forest, obeying an inner light and memory-trace, mother says to father, 'For God's sake, man, do something!'

So the father goes to the edge of the forest, and when the child is almost back, the father goes in the forest himself and howls like a wolf (and how well he howls, in his terror of the wolves – deeper here in the forest than ever before).

And his howling is so horrible, the child believes in it at once, and goes straight back home.

Finding Direction by a Star

The best thing of all is to get lost. So completely lost, you don't know where you're coming from, or where you're going.

Not more lost than a ship at sea, or an American without a buck, or a Calcutta beggar, or someone here, burning with desire, who longs to break the rules and wakes up looking for resources in himself.

The lost wanders completely lost till he comes into sight of himself and finally of other people. It's been said: find direction by a star, by the sun; feel your way in a fog, moss patch by moss patch.

Not everyone is up to the work. First you have to get lost.

Observations

A man was passed a hacksaw blade through his prison bars. He hid it in his clothes. For the rest of his life, he went about happily among the other prisoners.

The wedding cake was tall, thickly encrusted with marzipan and icing. The groom knew a file had been baked into it. At the reception, he saw the cake had been eaten up.

In the bridal chamber, sitting on the edge of the bed, sat the bride, her tongue moving over her lips, on which there were still traces of icing.

No one knows for sure whether the bride ever told the groom straight out what had happened to the file.

It's possible too that the man never asked. And it may be that, every day, without words, they shared their knowledge.

A Chat with the Plants

In the meadow I was chatting with the plants. I asked the questions, they answered.

'It's all meadow here, then the forest begins.'

'After we germinate, we rise from darkness: the world's wonderful - the sky glows with light! Then: cold! You can't retreat for shelter. And there's all these other hazards: trampling feet, downpours, thick shade from the trees, hard stones, grubs, diseases.'

The plants pointed out: 'From now on there's only one possible way back to seed: only one escape from evil: we must flower.'

A Seer's Despair

If a swimmer's got an anchor dangling from his thigh, it's nasty, crushing, to show him. He's bound to be using it for some important purpose. Not everything's what it seems.

If a person who says he's blind has only got his hat over his eyes, it's extremely hurtful, nasty, to show him. No one on earth shows anything to the blind, unless they want to be diabolically beastly.

If a hunter's got his gun the wrong way round and the barrel pressed to his forehead, someone would, for the sake of the children at least, certainly like to say something. But for God's sake! Surely a hunter, if anyone, knows how to use a shotgun?

A person astray on a dark road isn't looking for lostness or darkness.

'Health, yes. Just so much – not more! My head can't take it.'

Knowledge, a drop. Whoa, that's enough. You can chuck the rest.'

There has to be some limit. No dunce wants a teacher, and what stranger to his own illness wants a healer?

from **THE LAW** / LAKI (1989)

The Law

No one's daft – there are
people deprived of the wise,
people with their self-respect
knocked flat. No one's
hard – there are people with
hardened wounds.
No one's blind – there are
people cataracted by custom. Be different:
heal wounds and look up – wake
your darling out of sleep, hug her.
(We're all perfect.)

Cruel and Loving Judge

The creator of the world has to be a world.
The judge has to make the prison
perfect as an egg and incarcerate himself
for life. This is the secret of the mute swan's beak:
the creator of the wolf and the lamb
has to wolf down the lamb,
be crunched in the wolf's jaws.

Mistakes and Intimidation

Just fancy: somehow, through sheer daft youth,
someone manages a mistake – and is
schooled, intimidated, and shorn of error!

But error's what we're looking for – error to shear
perfection!

Poor you, to learn something here! Look,
here is the royal coach of your divinity,
the horse and the driver – all wrong,
so perfectly wrong, no one
but you can adore them, adopt them
and drive away – go, moreover,
wherever you want.

Grab Joy

The ocean's in motion: its moon-and-sun-motions
mark earth-time, moment-by-moment
vertical time.
Fish are in motion: they grow in the ocean,
sicken, expire, swim horizontally onward,
towards the death-mouth.

The sky's motionless, interminable:
the sea, for us, is merely a sport
and the fish-gurgle a giggle.

Icarus

Hearing a rumour of a break-out, they leak it
to the warders: not malice or treachery –
it's the only way to share
the break-out (to get away):

this, precisely, is how
they report their yearnings, and I mine.

Icarus has to fall – or the flight's not real:
Daedalus begot birds.

We let everything out, open our hearts and words, because
we're under lock and key

Escape Schemes

Idiots! And it's my fault – I should have been
more choosy. But what to choose from? – they've no notion
what trafficking in the soul means; the law grows
fast as grass, thicker than reeds: subsumes the lot.
These are my comrades in the get-away: That one
whoopees to the warders,
'We're on our way out!' This one
shows the governor his broken bars,
demanding gratitude for the workmanship.

I've only one hope: Soon, soon the whole staff'll
think us so daft we'll manage our getaway
through sheer lunacy.

Snakecharmer (Only Joy is Real)

Darling, sugar, no social reforms
can ever teach you joy, no universal
amnesty ever reach the ear of the warder
you ferry in your flesh, and no hospital
heal the angel guarding your heart.

You're human,
so pain teaches you speech, and when you walk in pain
speech is song, and when you sing, the serpent angel
slumbers off.

Genie

If only she'd accept the invitation, if
somehow I could learn to print her presence on my mind, if
somehow I'd the talent for an art with even an inkling
of the treasures her presence uncovers in me, let alone
learn the incantation of her lineaments, the cause
of all this happening, since she's physically real

I'd epiphanise the measureless riches within us,
burning our eyes into suns –

life's an unendurable metaphor for
knowing and yearning, knowing and surmising –

the seas rise towards the moon! a more diverting comparison
I can't find, the plants grow towards the sun,
tremble, turn in the terrible yearning.

The Beloved's Face

Because the greatest of these is love,
and because these are the features of love,
they'll never burn, though the frame burns:
never, through misdoing, amnesia, or mortality,
can you slash or foul this face –

its birth in you means utter forgiveness:
wipe out the world, it will remain.

It was born like a diamond
the earth-mother bore. The house will burn
but not burn this: your void life
slips off, but this face
is never effaced.

Explanations

A rose thinks four thoughts and always lives in them: This is seed, this is root, this is thorn, and this is flower. It never renounces the other thoughts for the sake of one – but man's only thought is flowering.

We're asleep. A writer's ability to depict the sleep shows the depth of our sleep. Kafka creates a colossus of sleep, and we swear to each other that he's shut in a solitary-confinement cell. Nothing's more painful than to imagine someone getting out of here and therefore seeing everything in fine detail.

Where was I supposed to be going, asks the unhappy taxi-driver. The fare's asleep, and the driver doesn't dare wake him. He's so afraid of the judgement in the morning ('you've not driven anywhere, where in hell are we?') that he kills the fare in his sleep.

HANNU MÄKELÄ

BORN 1943

TIMO VILJAKAINEN/OTAVA

Hannu Mäkelä is a prolific author, who has written 25 books, including novels, short stories and plays, since 1965, and has been a publisher's editor, and deputy head and head of the Finnish Literature Foundation. He has also edited several influential anthologies. A former teacher, and the son of teachers, he is well-known too for his popular children's stories about Herra Hu ('Mr Boo'). His searching, sometimes bitter, adult fiction portrays the cynicisms and betrayals of commercial society.

His dozen or so volumes of poems show Mäkelä as the exponent of the black midnight monologue, but also the joyous moment, and passionate contemplative absorption in the most everyday items and events. Born and for long employed in Helsinki, though now a freelance, he has a continual nostalgia for the country and retreats there whenever he can. There the most everyday items and events are carefully observed and gathered into pleasurable and painful enquiry and a quiet music. The atmosphere is a gently ecstatic melancholy, attentive to the fluctuations of Finnish land-

scape and weather, on the edge of depression, surviving through some intangible and impossible hope.

In his more recent work, the persona is hidden away in a cottage, with the great world seeming no more than a distant threat; the friend of birds and moths, he records the little details of life, the changes of light, the insects and tasks that encourage survival, though the nights may seem dark and long, and the cruelty of the seasons is inescapable.

The list of his titles summarises both his themes and his temperament.

POETRY BOOKS: *Sinisen taivaan, harmaan jään* (Blue Sky, Grey Ice) 1966, *Sano minulle nimesi* (Tell Me Your Name) 1969, *Vuoret ovat pilviä* (The Mountains are Clouds) 1972, *Vanha talo* (The Old House) 1973, *Syksy tuli kutsumatta* (Autumn Came Uninvited) 1974, *Jos pettää sinut elämä* (Should Life Deceive You) 1975, *Synkkyys pohjaton, niin myös iloni, onneni* (Gloom Infinite, and My Joy, My Happiness) 1976, *Illan varjo* (The Shadow of Evening) 1979, *Ikään kuin ihminen* (Just Like a Man) 1980, *Unelma onnesta numero 5* (Dream of Happiness Number 5) 1985, *Kylmä aika* (Cold Time) 1987, *Sinä teet pimeän, niin tulee yö* (You Make it Dark, and Night Comes) 1989.

from **THE MOUNTAINS ARE CLOUDS /** VUORET OVAT PILVIÄ (1972)

Picking cudweed and moon daisies
is a cruelty and extravagance
        comparable to
The Shitennoji Temple Gagaku Orchestra's
giddy collection of instruments.

from **GLOOM INFINITE, AND MY JOY, MY HAPPINESS /** SYNKKYYS POHJATON, NIIN MYÖS ILONI, ONNENI (1976)

You're born from smoke, from crepuscular love
it's made from heavenly birchbark, a hare's hair
that naked white of your skin
If there's a greater happiness, grab it
if black grief, dark pain
turn it towards my eyes
sustain the sound of the bass recorder
I'll screen you with my own skin
Life is a cut above death

The obscure cobwebs of your eyes
form from fresh-as-milk blind moon
If you love me more, then let me go
if you long for a tree, plant a festoon of vine
if a bird, take to the seashore
screen me with your skin
with the swarmings of your dark eyes
with the hoarse lust of honey
with night's full hips

from THE SHADOW OF EVENING / ILLAN VARJO (1979)

All night long a lamp lit
a white room. Cold. Sounds quieter
than breathing. And outside the window
a long dragging night waited
for morning's winding sheets
to come and cover the body: yes,
I was lying there full length, a daft king,
hands crossed on breast,
till morning when I must rise again
a briefcase among the briefcases.

At this station I'm not alone:
Everyone, following his fate,
contains a groan
that flutters flaglike in the wind
to the terror of the innocent.

Greyness, penetrating the voice.
A climate the spirit grows into
like a tightly buttoned jacket.
A reliable repeating time-signal.
A clearly readable comic strip.
A woman in whom you see
at once the tender moments,
the love, the inevitable parting.
You'll never meet her.

Money slipping through people's hands,
wearing thin, crushed, creased,
yet mightier than the miserable,
like a feather pillow
accidentally stopping a child's mouth…

Music is unearthly
but in heaven
no one sings. In the black clouds' rain
an oboe cry spreads in the room.
Evening
dark as wine. Night quiet.
You stare immobile into the dark.

from **DREAM OF HAPPINESS NUMBER 5 /** UNELMA ONNESTA NUMERO 5 (1985)

The sound that fills the room
is called music,
slow bows intone their joy
sombre as mourning,
the lamp stares amazed,
round, pregnant
with what can't be said.
I've lost my belief in progress
yet again, but not for a day
could I accommodate all alone
this body's needs for life.
I can only turn to the earth,
purchase the seed potato,
set it and hide it with soil:
so that something will rise and grow
that the grave deer will eat.

Noises I've not heard before.
An old house converses quietly,
but in the night outside too
someone is creeping by,
and as soon as I wake up
I see a large misty face at the window
that gradually melts into air.

Fear flutters me a moment,
but then I settle.
What to fear, I,
who've thought about death so long.
I think I hear the sound of someone pumping:
it's a wood warbler; then
a buzz in the electric wires:
but that too is only a bird.
And when I turn in bed
the door opens and shuts,
a floorboard creaks,
and someone walks lightly across the room,
but hasn't come to look as yet for me.

The small tortoiseshell has tried for weeks
to rise on her wings;
whenever I come, she's still there.
Though it's freezing out
she's eager for life,
and now I've found another under the bed.
I leave them water and honey,
but they don't want it,
merely move slowly
from place to place:
from window-ledge to radiator
to the chair's curved leg.
Something drives them on
though it seems so pointless.
There are still berries on the rowans,
birds in their hundreds,
bunching and dispersing, coming, going –
after food, what else?
Sawing logs, I'm tired out
as soon as I start.
How can you feel your uselessness
more clearly than that?
And yet, just looking out,
seeing the light greying in the dusk,
I understand you still have to deceive yourself a bit,
go on
with what you've been given.

She creeps very close in the night,
suddenly desiring nearness,
and I can't see why.
I just lie
unsleeping,
and try to be
the way she won't hear in her sleep
the black river flowing.

You there,
one woman and another,
and the moments that ease us
ever a little on our way.
Anyway, you,
no one else,
are so familiar, so new.

Narcotic snow drapes the house;
outside, wind wuthers,
and in the fireplace.
The lilacs flick a couple of dogged leaves;
catkins on the willows, even though
the river's only beginning its freeze.
I roam the well-known roads –
goodbye to the bushes and trees,
as so many times before;
I bow to the daydreams
I buried myself in
and inhabited for a moment.
Don't believe, don't trust, just live...
Dream and hope, wait and hope,
as it says at the end of the book:
the ships still move on the sea
if you find no place on earth.
Sometimes in mist sometimes in snow
I stand on the porch and stare,
as suits a ship's lookout.

How is the wind's tail?
Goodbye, goodbye, or maybe see you soon.
The wind freshens and gusts,
the sky's clearing:
a forecast good for the trip.
So the company's small, who cares?
To be together, for a bit, is the great thing.
Light's failing, though it's only three.
When the year's hinge turns
it's very black.
Have to go through the black to get to the open water.

CAJ WESTERBERG

BORN 1946

STEFAN BREMER/OTAVA

Caj Westerberg was born in the historic town of Porvoo on the south coast, the son of a detective inspector and a restaurant manageress. Now a freelance in Helsinki, he has studied in the United States, been a sailor, travelled to the Faroes, and lived in Denmark; he is bilingual in Finnish and Swedish; but all this suggests nothing of the acute sensitivity of his work.

For Westerberg, the poet is a truth-seeker and -speaker who tries to penetrate reality, but reality is nowhere but in the subjective experience – and may reveal itself particularly in the neglected experience.

What we are aware of *is* the world, but our very awareness and attentiveness alter it partially. The poet is both seer and fool, and his task is to be as aware as he can wherever he happens to be and record his sense-experience as observantly and attentively – and musically – as he can, looking at what may be overlooked.

This phenomenology is cool, timeless, minimalist, balancing the idiomatic and the stylised, with often surprising and witty associations.

In his tender and deliberate concentration on the evanescent experience and the moment of unfamiliarity, there may seem an implicit criticism of more political or social orientations to poetry. Yet equally implicit is a contempt for noisy concerns, money preoccupations and the "real world" of power and sterile action.

POETRY BOOKS: *Onnellisesti valittaen* (Happily Complaining) 1967, *Runous* (Poetry) 1968, *En minä ole ainoa kerta* (I'm Not the Only Instance) 1969, *Uponnut Venetsiä* (Drowned Venice) 1972, Äänesi (Your Voice) 1974, *Kallista on ja halvalla menee* (Dear and Going Cheap) 1975, *Reviirilaulu* (Territorial Song) 1978, *Elämän puu* (The Tree of Life) 1981, *Kirkas nimetön yö* (Bright Nameless Night) 1985, *Toteutumattomat kaupungit* (Unrealised Cities: Selected Poems) 1987.

from DEAR AND GOING CHEAP / KALLISTA ON JA HALVALLA MENEE (1975)

I'm in a café,
and outside the window
there's a small tree: a maple.
A fluttering of leaves.
Visible to the tip of its top.
Then, behind, though it seems in front,
a tram pulls up, stops, opens its throat
and bares its teeth.
Then the jaws clack shut and the whole contraption
slides off.
In the maple
there's a convulsion.

Buying and selling
selling and buying
our own life.
Bad, bad.
It's dear,
and it's going cheap.

She wondered if
she could ask me
to mow the lawn.
And I'm a person who
loves tall grass.
As snakes do.

from **TERRITORIAL SONG** / REVIIRILAULU (1978)

A seagull's shadow flaps across the gulf of the courtyard
and across the gone-sour yellow wall
gruesome and swift as a hanging;
that's how I'm dangling
from this moment in this city,
my ankle in a strangling noose
in the night, under the jangling stars, while over the roofs
a sheet-metal moon is rising
and blurred dreams are yawning in a thousand windows;
down below, the city,
and in my breast the heart is socking
like a knuckleduster.

The simplest noise,
the noise of a glass
when you put the glass down
on a wooden table, the sound of wood
on glass
        is like
a flash of happiness
on a sad face.

The clock looks
accusingly at me:
evening's here already,
and I can't help asking,
What is this debt and whom do I owe it to?

Oh I do: I owe it.
All day long I've been digging in my mental pockets,
and it's depressing: nothing there,
except sentimental small change.
Nothing's burning,
there's no Acropolis lucid

against a Mediterranean blue sky.
No black ache of a doorway, either, thank God.
No sheep-scamper of panic.
And no light-rapier from eternity –
no blinding spectre
impaling a water drop
on the young cheek of an apple. Oh no.

As I look out of a bus window in a slight mist and a light snow
let's hope a craving for ecstasy will be fed by
that stack of coal on the wharf:
the poor man's Kilimanjaro.

Bits of macaroni on the floor.
A lapful of bawling snotty child,
and something eluding me
is lingering
and not shaping into words:
guessed at, on the edge of breaking.
And when I switch the radio on, a performance of
Dmitri Shostakovich

comes like the butterfly
that wandered
into the foyer of the Restaurant de l'Univers,
that evening of September sun,
its wings
splashing with light.

Behind the gauzy trees
light out of cloud.
Brains squeezed by silence.

It won't open up,
not into speech, that flaring van Gogh: the March willows,
the colour of the water:

the clean street of the eye
through the thick consciousness of the cornfield.

It won't open up, your hand,
enough to make a resting place for a working eye: like
stepping into cool water.

Night. Stars. We're ready
courteously
to take off
each other's
skin.

Flirtation? Sparrow
as peacock. Seedcracking eaglebeak!
Or the peacock itself
pitifully parading, here among the writhing bumps
of the pine roots. On stony soil, among cranberry sprigs.
Now anyway
the sparrows are snickering, can't be seen,
with the January sun already peeping
into the hawthorn hedge. And the wooden wall of the old city's
taking off towards us as a smell.

Always I drop into being a child.
I always fell into playing a girl: here's my heart,
a cobblestone,
or cloddish
as a mashed-up sandpie.

If you want to hear
what you want to hear
say it yourself.
My poetry's not a prayer wheel.
My heart's no placard either.
Worn-out stuff, perhaps,
worn-through in several places.

And a poem –
let's think of it as a red pall:
to wound living eyes
and drape over the dead.

from **THE TREE OF LIFE** / ELÄMÄN PUU (1981)

This is a sandpit all right:
a tree or two,
a climbing frame,
a roundabout, and swings,
and on a concrete post
in red chalk
a text:

A GROWNUP
CANT KNOW
WHAT YOUNG
        LOVE
        IS

A dry alder leaf drifts
on water seeming to echo silence.
Your face looks out of our empty room
as if from a mirror,
mingled with sky and birches.
And now you open the door, and cool damp comes in with you
as you drop your burdens on the floor.

There's wood in the basket, newspaper on the wood.
You fetch the matches from the mantelpiece.
When the fire's going you settle in.
You take a book from your bag, a pen and a pad.
You start to read. Make notes. Read.
As dark comes, you sit a while looking out
at the luminous lake.

I'd like to get up,
cross the floor,
and dial
your number.

from **BRIGHT NAMELESS NIGHT** / KIRKAS NIMETÖN YÖ (1985)

First of all
from childhood
an image and a scent
coming from wooden porch-steps in the sun.
I haven't,
it occurs to me,
often been in later years
so right with the world.
Then the picture begins to move:
I imprisoned a fly in my palm.
I tore its wings off.
Watched
its funny walk on the hot steps.

The bird doesn't know
how it soars or sings.
The crocus doesn't know how violet glows.
The girl doesn't know how to look, how to look;
or if she does, you'd better
turn your eyes away, or it'll all
get complicated.

A man with an expression
like the National Theatre
and the girl going by
goes by

How wide the eyes have to be
to see the world

The eyes open: the room's filled
with new light.
I draw back the curtain: it's snowing out.
Ahead: the day's work.
Into what's still unseen
there's already travelling
another light.

The sedimented
fluid of the world's brain
whose murk we wade through –
just now by a canal bank.
On a crust of lightly snow-dusted ice
a pigeon's clawprints.

The lake settles into the night
without a shiver:
a forest mirror sucking the sky deep in.
A lone-flying woodcock
pencils a *frisson* of shadow on the water's skin.
Your skin
shudders now.

As the dark fingers your hair
I want to sit and sit here
on this cooling rock.
I want to watch the stars
pulsing nearer and nearer
and the travelling lights of the distant ships.

JARKKO LAINE

BORN 1947

KAI NORDBERG KY/OTAVA

Born into a working-class family – his mother delivered newspapers – **Jarkko Laine** grew up in Turku on the west coast and in the sixties formed part of a Finnish 'beat' movement there. He is still largely centred on Turku but, without losing his irreverence and humour, lives the life of a man of letters and writes novels, plays and criticism as well as poetry. After nearly twenty years as Editorial Secretary of *Parnasso*, Finland's foremost literary magazine, he became Editor-in-chief in 1987. Since 1988 he has been chairman of the Finnish Writers' League. In 1980 he formed part of the International Writers' Programme in Iowa.

Laine is a satirist motivated by a hatred of poetry, at least conventional poetry, and religion. Many of the poets in this volume are implicitly mocked in his surrealistic parodies, and so are the sayings of the wise. 'Without cynicism, it's impossible to live' is probably Laine's own philosophy; and he would recommend 'Learn cynicism, and take up thy bed, and walk', if he did not know it is unwise to give advice.

His early work had affinities not only with the Beats but with

Whitman, and he assimilated many features of mass and pop culture. He has produced some hilarious novels. It was in the 1970s that he changed his persona, revealing himself as the critical and culturally sophisticated writer he really is. He can let himself go at length, but increasingly he has been writing epigrammatic records of a not uncheerful disenchantment. *Life is a Rented Room* – aptly, it seems – is the title of one of his books. Significantly, he has translated Anthony Powell and Mark Twain, among others.

POETRY BOOKS: *Muovinen Buddha* (Plastic Buddha) 1967, *Tulen ja jään sirkus* (The Circus of Fire and Ice) 1970, *Niin se käy* (That's How it Goes) 1971, *Nauta lentää* (The Cow Flies) 1973, *Valitut runot* (Selected Poems) 1975, *Viidenpennin Hamlet* (Fivepenny Hamlet) 1976, *Paratiisi* (Paradise) 1978, *Elämä on vuokrahuone* (Life is a Rented Room) 1980, *Amerikan cowboy* (American Cowboy) 1981, *Villiintynyt puu* (A Tree Gone Wild) 1984, *Elokuvan jälkeen* (After the Cinema) 1986, *Traagisen runoilijan talo* (A Tragic Poet's House) 1986, *Runot 1967-1987* (Collected Poems 1967-1987) 1987, *Oodi eiliselle sanomalehdelle* (Ode to Yesterday's Newspaper) 1989.

from **PLASTIC BUDDHA** / MUOVINEN BUDDHA (1967)

Plastic Buddha

You could say: ‘A lamp post is a tree
                    that bears brilliant fruit.’
And walk to the end of the street where the fields begin
                                        and the row of lamps ends,
      stand with the whole forest of lights behind you,
and dark night in your eyes, lukewarm coffee.

Why don’t you say. Why don’t you count cobblestones
                                        like your shoes do.
The moon you could touch from the roof. The stars are distant.

When the hair grows over the collar, the face is unshaven
   and crapula is bloodshot under the eyelids:
and a car arrives in consciousness, Packard or Bentley,
                                        makes no difference,
                 and plastic flows along the pavement.

It takes the form of Buddha.

He sits, as morning dawns, in the lotus position.

In his cupped palms he has a string of streetlamps,
      at his feet a prayerwheel throbs like a car engine,
and he says: ‘On the primus the water boils.’

The wind grabs the girls’ skirts and whips them off.
On the beach a hand gropes out of the sand.
You feel bad and the words elude you.

The smoke bows over the rooftops.

A mandala has been inscribed round the bus.
The bus windows are crusty with July hoarfrost.

The lamp-posts, you notice, have wilted.
The iron withers and the glass fades.

from **THE CIRCUS OF FIRE AND ICE /**
TULEN JA JÄÄN SIRKUS (1970)

The Bodhisattva's 177th Saying

The huge train weeps in the night
& the platform asks:

'Why, O locomotive, are you weeping?'

'I'm shattered, I'm shattered:
the track's too long,
        to lick up
            at one go.'

When the Streets Change Colour

When the streets blanch,
                        as five seasons go,
I'll remember you
                            in this city
        where shadow shuns shadow.

It's all over, I know,
I'm packing my bag,
                            and ready again to go,

I'll be back when the timetables swap,
    when the clock's still asleep,

I'll tap on your door, not pound,
                            in this city street
            where sound is scared of sound.

My Lollipop Lolita

With the electrolier off
she read comic strips
under the sheets.
by torchlight

And as I got out of my long johns
she was giggling
at the balloon texts.

What was I supposed to do?
When I pulled back the quilt
she thrust the light in my eye.
I tried to worm on top of her
and she slapped my cheek with her comic.

Christ, I thought,
Catch me being a Charlie!
I pulled the quilt off her
and cried: 'Aha! Lothar!'
'The invaders shall be shot down!'
'The Cobra will never surrender!'

She rolled on her back, laughing.
Her pyjama top hutched up to her breasts.
'Great! Great!
Just like Mick Magic.'

I reached for my coat and trousers,
put my shoes on
and went out in the yard.

I was The Wounded Man of Åbo,
The Turk from Turku.
I fell full length on the icy street.
A lamp hissed overhead.

The Goodbyes

The café lights are out,

The one-armed bandit's dingdong
has become a siren's wail:

in the park stand
statues of cloth –

silent dummies
the pubs have stuffed;

on the deserted street
a car sets itself alight.

Ode to the Moon

O Moon!
In the sky's dark bathroom
Thou art The Plug!

O Moon!
On the blue blazer of night
Thou art the brass button!

O Moon!
In the department store of dreams
Thou art the stopped lift!

O Moon!
Mr Universe!
Thou chawest scrap iron like a tobacco quid!

O Moon!
Thou art a thumbmark
On the window-pane of space!

O Moon!
Charming banana-boy
The clouds watch thee, eager for a nibble!

O Moon!
Raised baseball-catcher's glove
Catch! Catch!

O Moon!
To thee we sacrifice our science!
Our money! Our all!

O Moon!
Thy cheeks are healthy!
No hunger in thee!

O Moon!

O Moon!

O Moon!

from **THAT'S HOW IT GOES** / NIIN SE KÄY (1971)

Has Someone Won Already?

1

Only at night, with the water black,
does the river mirror the factory.

As a salesman rolls out a cloth
the ripples roll the factory image out.

The sky has many stars.
Their light has staying power.

2

My watch changes the date suddenly,
for that's how it's made:
the days short,
the hours long.

Every hour music from the radio
        that I attend to like a seismograph;
    I sit on the floor of my room
  and think how wrong it is
  that the brains hog so much blood:
much more than my toes,
which are cold.

3

I deny anything still exists.
I deny some catastrophe will be universal.
I deny the heart can play the conductor right off the podium.
I deny the mouth is mud.
I deny the earth is someone's.

For who would declare war now?
It'll merely be continued.

The waves are fleeing the rocks.
After pounding them for millennia
they've understood it doesn't work.

Now they're assaulting the sea
as if to curb its raging.

4

Sometimes I warm to the thought
that the globe is not a sort of crustacean
and the space around us merely a hard
transparent plastic.

Above, there's first a bubble of air.
Then the thoughts of Einstein.
But our history is not even a fossil's history.

We're a souvenir. A piece of life
encased in plastic,
held in a soft hand
whose fingers are unpredictable.

5

(and the pollution of nature, is it not God's will?
 a new manifestation of his grace?

we shall endure.
mankind shall not perish.

we shall live in iron lungs
and kidney machines. it is true.

but what nobler task could there be for man,
the created, than to armour with his own technology
the divine miracle of his own body
breathed into life from the dust?)

6

SUPPORT THE PEOPLE OF VIETNAM
bank giro no:
419522-5,55800

7

Plastic brush in mouth,
I stand before the mirror,
foam on my chin
and sore shoulders beneath my shirt.

This morning a colourless water
flows down the window-pane
and stops on the peeling wood.
This morning my hope.
I keep silence
and no one answers.

My teeth
sink in my gums
sink in white bread
as my sorrow
into sorrow and into flesh
and again and again.

My face
is in the mirror
as if somewhere in the unknown

from whose origin
we learn nothing but speculation
and whose history
is profounder than my history,
like the rain,
the water,
grief,
this morning and the silence.

from THE COW FLIES / NAUTA LENTÄÄ (1973)

When you're stripped of everything,
brought to your knees
and pinned down there,
you don't get up and fight.
You grind your teeth, get drunk,
and feel that life has betrayed you.

If Calvin for God, why not me for Marx,
the man thought, intelligent, well-bred.
He pranced up to the poor: 'Good morning, poor!
I'm your friend, I decided to come and help you.'
They made room for him, no questions asked.

He settled in, had his library brought,
sharpened his pencil and entered the struggle,
struggled tirelessly, was content.

The poor got on with their lives, did their chores,
since they have to watch out for themselves.
But the man – he struggled in a fever all night long:
only in the morning did he straighten his back, and gaze
towards the horizon.
'It's The Dawn already!' he shouted.
And indeed the sky was reddening.

Morning broke. The poor picked up their nosebags,
went their separate ways to the day's work.

At the dinner break, up comes The Perfect In-mate:
'It's The Dawn, comrades! Support the United Front!'

from **PARADISE** / PARATIISI (1978)

A Shout from Two Storeys Down

I've been taking a look at myself in other people –
as they scissor through the world
to get to another, better world,
screwing themselves without end
and giving their eyelids no rest.

The grip on life
is comprehensive but limp.
It's a ramble through a familiar landscape
by an unfamiliar route.

The oaths sworn in youth,
the arrows in the hunter's hand,
can be chucked away at the end of the day
like a bird-battened sheaf of wheat.

from **A TREE GONE WILD** / VILLIINTYNUT PUU (1984)

The gilt is peeling off the idol,
but not implying any apostasy:
it's proof of the devotees' faith:
scratch your god,
and you prove the size of your faith.

A daubed block was all right
till the gilder had finished his job.
And legend tells us:
when the block was thrown away,
it wept blood.

April snow is smutty:
the dads have been wiping their razors
on the pavement edges.

The sons trudge childhood's street,
wound in by silence.

At the way's end
it's a Pilgrim's Way.

The last zoological garden
has been painted
on the bomb shelter wall:

it's a concrete picture of Eden
intended for no one's eyes.

I climbed a rhinoceros's back –
or was it a grey and level
motorway?

I saw exotic landscapes,
and heard a canary sing
in a street of rain;

smashed shop windows
looted by the poor,
who were snatching TVs,
like Prometheus snatching fire;

the daydreams they raise
are streaming banners;
but they themselves are waiting
with no heads raised.

Monday Morning

Pencil drawings, both faith and doubt
left under a wet jacket-sleeve.

The town wakes,
and light goes on in the Pathology Department's windows.

Yet from the *Umbra et pulvis*...
Yet from the dust you get instant-man:
just add a cupful of black coffee and stir,
and he sits up again, moaning about his lot.

The frontal bone's a strong bastion:
beyond lies the barbarian land.

So Goodbye, John Keats

The West...is it the one the Egyptian dead
journey to, or the one Stetson-hatted hombres
riddle each other in with six-shooters?
No matter, really. It's where the sun goes down,
behind the trees, and then it's dark. And even if
beauty is indeed in the eye of the beholder, the eye
no longer sees it. The room's no longer here,
or the book of poems we were reading: merely
a thing in stiffened hands. So short
the light, and art so short.

So goodbye now, John Keats.
The dark is pullulating like a microscope slide,
but we're too high, too magnified.

From the Book of the Wise

Beneath a large umbrella
sits Gautama,
a fat man in a white frock:

'To attain truth, restrain your hand.'

'Guruji, say more.'

'Without cynicism, life is impossible.
Yet it is unwise to say to every cripple,
"Take up thy bed and walk".'

ILPO TIIHONEN

BORN 1950

TIMO KIRUS / WSOY

Ilpo Tiihonen comes from the north, Kuopio, where his father was a postmaster and his mother a post office clerk. He is now a freelance in Helsinki, and his poems are set in the Helsinki streets, shops, station, pubs and blocks of flats.

Tiihonen makes use of rhyme, unlike most of the poets in this volume, creating an ironically slanted lyrical satire, whose cynical defences do not disguise a fundamentally romantic emotion.

He could be accused of sentimentality. Nostalgia and affection are often at the base of his poems, however much they veer to comedy, surrealist perspectives or nonsense. He has an extraordinary affection for drunks. He feels the poignancy of lame dogs, and appears to aim emotionally below the belt. More often than not he doesn't succeed in arousing a comparable feeling – assuming he is sincere in his wish for the apotheosis of the down-and-out. Rather, the reader becomes an amused accomplice willing to go along with and look at his 'concern', experiencing more comedy than empathy.

But at least he is trying something new after three Finnish decades of privately felt perceptions in non-metrical aphoristic lines. Begun as a necessary corrective to an earlier comfortable conformity, the turn-around can now perhaps benefit from new directions, and new directions tend to be the rediscovery of older ones – in this case the Russian and Swedish classics. Ultimately, too, memorable lines are often facilitated by rhyme and metre, or at least modifications of them.

Tiihonen writes colloquially, uses slang liberally, and his voice is very distinctive, suggesting both a lively daring mind and an emotional life open to the temptations he satirises.

He has been influenced by Mayakovsky, Yesenin and Gustav Fröding. His first play was having a successful run in Helsinki in Spring 1990.

POETRY BOOKS: *Sarkunmäen palo* (Sarkunmäki Fire) 1975, *Teille ei tarjoilla enää* (We Can No Longer Serve You) 1978, *Arjen armada* (Everyday's Armada) 1980, *Eroikka* (Eroica) 1982, *Hyvät, pahat ja rumat* (The Good, the Bad and the Ugly) 1984, *Enkelin tavara* (Angel's Things) 1986, *Taivaan kulmilla* (At the Corners of the Sky: Selected Poems) 1987, *Ei-Kaj Plumps. Hyppyjä Helsinkiin* (Noperhaps Plumps. Jumps into Helsinki) 1989.

from **EROICA** / EROIKKA (1982)

Sitting in the Baron's Lap

Though the sofa's holey
and the springs ring
and long lost youth is shaking
like the flesh's last fling

she's dancing, she's delicious
in her neckerchief's silk
naked and flagitious
and soft as buttermilk

and the Hungary of dreams
is sending out gleams
and night's soft muzzle
is beginning to nuzzle
the lids of her eyes
and crop the twilight from her thighs

And the Baron in his Bentley
is coming through the plums
and the moon's on her bosom
which so easily succumbs

and the twisting damp staircase
is suddenly space

She's dancing naked
and let her burning go
down storeys storeys storeys
and out into the snow

through the Danube's thick bubblings
and into the mists
galloping off from all troublings
with curls and twirling wrists

till far below
the passing stranger
demon fiddler with whirling bow
will throw a bottle
and scatter her in the snow.

So from the courtyard
she must get up and go
slowly dragging back to the home of woe –

the kitchen table
to plug away
at the football coupon
and that half-carafe
still left
of Hungarian rosé.

Baby

Later on
when moored behind Dream Crag
our boneboat bobs in the darkening bay
and the water rat (perhaps Old Ratty)
still prints his paw memoranda
in the wet clay

in our third thousand years
the horizon's laurel
will tangle your dreaming ears

and without waking you
this poem left here
by your cot perhaps caress your hair.

from **THE GOOD, THE BAD AND THE UGLY /**
HYVÄT, PAHAT JA RUMAT (1984)

Afternoon

When the great master dyer
    rinses your grey hair
    with henna tears,
dusting the Kalahari of your face
    with the flying hooves of years

you'll hardly be startled
    if that someone you've addressed –
    The End of the Paragraph –
swings in the swing door
slightly embarrassed
    at coming across the floor

with the hairdresser's dryer
    playing adagio
    in a hot hi-fi flow
and an afterimage from your chair
blows a smoke ring
    to hover in the air

Dirty Angel

The angel of night loiters on the stairs
waiting in the rear
pack on back
and digging with her dirty nail
in her pretty ear

she's come with a consignment
of eternal hot water and beds
supplies of teeth and legs
and strong nerves for nervous people
who've lost their heads

and this is the way this Christmas Eve:
at eleven fifty-seven:
the dustbins burst with loud reports
and a hundred drunks who're not expecting
are resurrecting
with no passports
straight into heaven.

Weighing Machine

Eric's sleeping contentedly
on the railway station.
Has visited the off-licence. The smell of mountain ash
permeates early June
and yet far away
thunder is gathering.

Into the Black Maria
Constable Niiranen
is hoisting his dear old dad
and wondering

how the days
can grow heavier
even though his dad, old Eric,
punctually
day by day
is
on the contrary
getting lighter.

ARTO MELLERI

BORN 1956

KAI NORDBERG KY/OTAVA

Arto Melleri, a shopkeeper's son, was born in Lappajärvi in Ostrobothnia on the west coast, and his contemporary urbanism still suggests a feeling of exile. He often recalls the agricultural life, resorting to it for lurid and far from reassuring imagery, though his often savage vigour is sometimes modified by affectionate lyrical moods.

He studied at the Finnish School of Drama and has been a literary adviser to several theatres. He was part-author of *Pete Q*, an avant-garde hit play of 1987, which established the point of view of the new theatrical generation. His play *Sopimus Mr Evergeenin Kanssa* ('Contract with Mr Evergreen') was published in 1983.

He worked in an experimental group that liberated the theatre of the seventies from political dogmatism. He reacted against both idyllic miniatures and Marxism in his poetry. Nevertheless he is haunted by man's political inhumanity, remembers the crimes of yesterday, today and tomorrow, and reports them in a prophetic

apocalyptic rhetoric whose panache alone prevents it sounding like despair.

He attacks Zola as a new-style writer of a media age, and invokes the poets of the past as alternative sources of insight and guides to truth. Truth, and the decadence resulting from the betrayal of truth, are continual concerns in his highly-charged outpourings of scathing imagery.

Melleri began writing in a series of story-confessions 'by the young', intended for teenagers. This slightly embarrassing, if live-wire, beginning got him off to an early start, however, and he developed into the leading figure in 'the new subjectivism' of his generation.

POETRY BOOKS: *Meno-paluu* (There and Back) 1970, *Liftarien yö* (Hitcher's Night) 1973, *Schlaageriseppele* (A Garland of Pop-Songs) 1978, *Zoo* (Zoo) 1979, *Ilmalaiva 'Italia'* (The Airship 'Italia') 1980, *Mau-Mau* (Mau Mau) 1982, *Johnny B. Goethe* (Johnny B. Goethe) 1988, *Nuoruus, siivekästä ja veristä: Runot 1972-1989* (Youth, Winged and Bloody: Collected Poems 1972-1989) 1989.

from **A GARLAND OF POP-SONGS** / SCHLAAGERISEPPELE (1978)

That Boy

That boy whose nails were always black,
whose hair was always straggling in his eyes,
that boy ate chalk, drank ink,
    sneered every time the teacher
turned his back to signalise on the map
    where the famous lakeside route went, where
        the Swedish border was: that boy
sneered and ate chalk and washed it down
                    with ink.
In the break, behind the woodpile,
    he planned to draw the world's largest
        picture of a cunt,
            football-field-sized, with chalk sidelines.
He fell in the cesspool in spring
        up to his waist
but didn't cry. Not that boy.
    Waited for the sun to dry his trousers,
        his only ones. That boy.

Germania

At a stone table
a pale Mendelssohn, a perspiring Wagner.
The concert's finished, both are quiet.
All this we know from history,
hacked in the mountainside, and from music,
a plague of cricket-chirpings.
The cities were built of gingerbread-hearts
        and violin strings.
Hides were flayed from wild beasts.
Wine was trodden from unripe grapes
        with big boots.
Millions queued in the shut stations
        as if entraining;

death was unmentionable: the whole line, sleeper after sleeper,
the engine, the plume of steam and the firefly-dance of sparks
                    under the sweating silk of night.
Later, we heard – history told us
with its festering mouth and rotten teeth:
The giant needed a deluge
for a facewash before turning his back
                    and sleeping again.
The Grimm brothers, there were only two, but nightmares
more than writers to pen them.
Up the mountain an eagle is still brooding
                    on a stone egg,
and down below in the villages
                    the alarm bells clang;
the engine-whistle slashes the mist of sleep –
the whole trip I slept
in the wrong compartment between two fat ladies,
the whole trip, and this is Cologne.

In Greece Death Is No Shade

1

That summer, Europe's motorways
      glued to the scorched earth
         a charred wind.
I crossed the frontier at night, morning pitched me
on a white-hot hardness,
      a treeless flatland:
it was as quiet as if the history-long working day
were over and the old men
      were collecting dried newspapers
         in the continent's cemeteries.
Sheep, gone wild, were wandering through the ruins,
      their baaings like
         heavily falling snow:
no one was shearing the sheen of their fleece.
And death is no shade
      but a sun that melts a cast of white gold
         on the earth-crust's stony aching collar-bones;

sun death blared sulphurous flames,
    like a mute trumpet-section;
here the fathers' good and bad works
    are all equally good
        and nothing gives you to understand
            that one is happier than the other,
                the earth than the sea,
                    or you than me.

2

In the evening I was in Athens,
    and in an Italian restaurant,
        I was eating spaghetti and drinking
            a Greek beer: FIX.
Suddenly it began to rain
    as if the old city
        were taking a shower
            after the history-long working day.
It began to rain,
    and the chapel bell began to beat,
        hollowly, whanging,
            as if even history was yawning,
but I was so famished
I ordered another helping a minute later.

Zola

The mirror denies itself.
I deny the mirror.

1

'I thirst for the pox, and the plague,
which inflame ever-barren beauty's
philoprogenitive itch between the thighs:
let me linger a little as a trembling
body hair on your scabby skin,
                        O truth, truth –'

2

The poet
  out of the mirrors' reach
    with the daemon in his goosequill

pierced his rough paper
before the time of the telegraph,
before the telegraph lines crossing the continent:
the news had time
to hang itself a thousand times
on every pole.

The poet
lit by his secret lantern
did what your brilliant gaslight
could never accomplish, Émile.
You were the scurry of molecules,
the bubble of the chemical compound
in the arsenic-green glass,
you metamorphosed the mirror-frame's roses
into snakes
and thought the image itself was changing:
yes, thought, and your sort thinks so still.

3

You and your sort
think truth's a whore
who's stripped off
her whalebone corsets.
Truth beds with many men
but takes no money
nor loses her maidenhead.
The radiotelegraph and the photograph
have told more lies
than perspectiveless painting
or the gossip steaming
in old biddies' skirts from washhouse to washhouse.
I deny the mirror, the photograph and the telegraph,
your holy trinity, Émile.
Once the wind gets up
it wipes the smuts away
from factory girls' complexions.
Moonlight sweeps bare the garbaged yard.
Sunrays rinse
the gloomy room's black mirrors.
You and your sort
scrabble in vain in the streets
for the splinters of your mirrors.

from **ZOO** / ZOO (1979)

Spirits of the Marsh

The moon casts its spawn
in the green water: Hecate, a bloodshot light,
a caul on the earth.
I'm just leaving.
The marsh listens to me, the marsh spirits,
the mist, the birds of prey whoop
in trees dried into sticks.

Many have left, the marsh has taken many
horses and men. Sometimes, before
your bootprints are sucked smooth,
a bright drop of water
spills in the mud, the failing light
refracts in it, and then marsh is marsh again,
night night, the ways of those who've gone before
inscrutable as ever.

I listen to the marsh: dreamspun wool
will soon float the meadows. The marsh has taken
many horses and men, the junipers
are crouching along like Birnam Wood.
I edge along, cautiously, groping;
the marsh listens to me, without breathing.
A drop of bright water!
Too little to wash your hands in.

Apocrypha

This Venice is doomed –
      to sink, to drag with it
the dancing candle flames, the tatty delights
      of silken ribbons.

The four-poster fortifications
were set up to fight philandering,
the senses were routed
on wildernesses of Persian carpets.
Tonight wild horses
are whinnying, the moonlight is ploughing
blue shadows in the snow.

The assembly rooms have been papered
with ashes, and sealed from the wind
to stop ideas breathing
air. I'm going with no goodbye, orientating
by the disposition of the stars
on the night of Trotsky's murder.
The world's a pile of collapsed histories, a pile
of inkstained explanations why.
Everything now being published is apocryphal.
The revolution has begun already, the first prisoners
have been taken: they're going round and round
an unshadowed yard, heads shaved,
hands behind heads, their shoelaces undone.

After the Ball

Some day every pleasure-dome turns into
an underground dungeon, dawn
casts on the French chalk
the shadow of a grill.
This time the make-up won't wash off,
and for the last waltz you must always
bring your own shackles...over the congealed
wine-puddles, the broken glass, the torn-up
visiting cards:
the counts and viscounts you met in the evening
have lost their estates by morning.

All you can bring to the last waltz
   are your own shackles, and those you have to dance with
                                        till you drop,
or else renounce them, blow the candles out,
        and sleep head down on the marble table,
to stop you hearing: tomorrow
          is crashing down in front of you
             like the gate of Spandau.

Blue Eve

Strange sheets
easily seem shrouds
when crapula flashes
the room blue: cold light,
the glint of guillotine steel.

Before the head drops
the mouth mumbles something, learned by rote,
but the light does not flinch; everything
it pierces, and I know:
there are twelve ribs
for the heart to bruise itself against.

From one of them Eve was made,
a blue woman, her mount
formed from clay. Strange
sheets easily seem
shrouds when everything's going
round: the merry-go-round
turns executioner's wheel…One after another
the ribs crack.
But the light does not flinch.

from **THE AIRSHIP 'ITALIA'** / ILMALAIVA 'ITALIA' (1980)

Summer, Cruel and Totally Innocent

Summer goes by holding
its breath, the shrubbery rustles
with lovers' mosquito-bitten passions,
grass crushed under their naked flesh, and aspen leaves
mimicking the heart's flutterings.
Unripe strawberries: June is cruel, and totally innocent.
Summer goes by holding
its breath, short-breathed, and soon a long groan is heard
from the misty evening's accordion;
bright lights patrol the black fields,
leaving a prickly stubble, and the sky
drops lead drop after lead drop;
the strawberries rot, the scarecrow
stands among blackened ruins of willowherb,
and the spirit of the bankrupt farm's owner
sets up home in it.

Summer's gone.
At the edge of the abandoned strawberry field
the farmer spreads his hands, his torn pockets.

In March a child is born.

Night-piece Against Witches

On Easter night a forest full of the bawling of wounded cattle
rises and circles the village, dancing, dancing,
in the smoke of bonfires.
The flood-water mirrors April's nickel.
The churned-up roads are
printed with cracked hooves.

In winter everything's frozen but madness,
but now it's spring, the time
for fulfilling of curses.

Still the eager sprigs thrash the smoke, the old Michelins
smoulder on in their ash-drifts until dawn.
In the draughty attic drifts a surge of sawdust.
In the house of man no one can sleep.

Folksong

A frosty night, and the shadow of a snipe
        bleats over the estate, in the bridal farmyard
stiff grass gleams with blood

Instead of the bride corpse-shrouds
        on the bridal bed, and in the stable
a muzzle snatches at the moon

Ten years more and the bridegroom
        will be back from Vaasa gaol, till then
how a palliasse can prick at night

The Marks of Little Dirty Hands

I gaze out of a curtainless window
a child has pressed his little dirty
                                        hands on, standing
on a chair and waiting for his mother to come.
Tumbles.

A spring day, a blinder.
Mesmeric suggestion is what maintains
world order: in the beginning
was the Covenant with the Devil, at the end
the Balance of Terror.
The forest stands silent against the haze of frost.

I gaze out of a curtainless window.
We've no hope
to squander.

SATU SALMINIITTY

BORN 1959

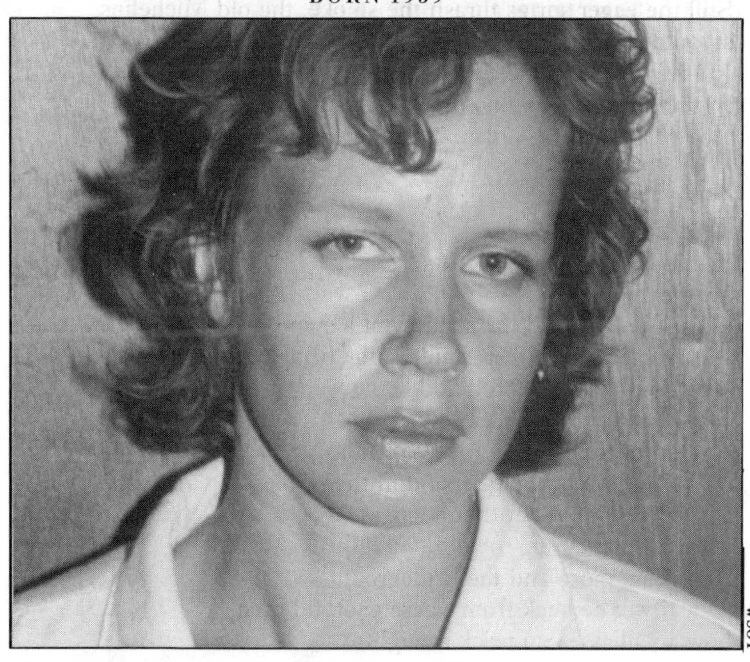

WSOY

The youngest poet here, **Satu Salminiitty** can only be compared to Ahti in her blend of the erotic, the earthy and the metaphysical, though the two poets are utterly different. Her rhetorical rhythms and idioms, distanced from the spoken idiom, are incantations of prayer and praise. Water and dissolving are familiar mystical images, and here a strong personality is relishing the surrender of itself in the ecstasies of love. Her unfashionably optimistic confidence in life and death is based on an implicit criticism of rationalism. Her otherworldliness is not a withdrawal but a refusal to separate otherworldliness from this-worldliness. It enhances her sensuality and fervour for intense experience.

She is perhaps a type more familiar in seventeenth-century and romantic English poetry, though her idiom is a new invention. One can't help admiring her frankness and her bold rejection of a timid, respectable and conformist agnosticism. It will be interesting to see how she sustains her vision.

POETRY BOOKS: *Aikataika* (Timespell) 1981, *Paratiisiaavistus* (Presentiment of Paradise) 1983, *Elämän huoneet* (Life's Rooms) 1986, *Raottuvien ovien valo* (Light Through Slightly Opening Doors) 1989.

from **PRESENTIMENT OF PARADISE / PARATIISIAAVISTUS (1983)**

Image of God

What would you do
with no looking-glass, photo,
or reflection?
                    Whom would you hand
a pen to and say, 'Draw me!'
                              Which water would be
calm enough, worthy of credit,
which eyes
                 accepting enough?

In death you can no longer contemplate yourself.
Therefore
you can see God.

Supreme Spell

Perhaps no bad idea
to loll
deep down in a hollow
                    and admire
the grass-stalk trapezists
and calculate the speed of the clouds – perhaps

no bad idea, to lie
on the aquamarine sky,
on the night's lead and charcoal…

ALPHA AND OMEGA!

Round us would buzz
more mesmerising than the multiconurbations
                                        the huge

root-universe, its
soft live squashiness like skin, ah!
skinlike... ALPHA! and all around us would mutter
                                        the skull-mumblings of gone minds, oh
                                        the consensus of insatiable worms:
                                                                        OMEGA!

                                        In the Kingdom of Harmony
the symbiosis of bone and mould...

But perhaps, for all that,
it would be no bad idea
to be that humus, that plush velvet:
ALPHA AND OMEGA
ALPHA, OMEGA
ALPHA
OMEGA

Healing Water

His face has the lightness
of water, there's a skytrack
in his laughter, I travel
the highway of his teeth, his lips,
to the earnestness of lust,
into death.

But the water bobs with games, it's affluent,
healing water
spilling kid-stuff horseplay. I reach for
his hair:
          it spreads
like seaweed
             tranced, free-flowing,
gusty, sailing

is this craving
for the man I love.

from **LIFE'S ROOMS** / ELÄMÄN HUONEET (1986)

His long lashes hurt me,
his freedom in his dreams
                    shocks my heart.

I'd like to suck his penis and weep
and he'd push his hands in my hair, he'd grope there, his eyes
would darken.

Sleep, sleep.

We live in such a weird world –
eyes have to be closed to stop them
burning, melting.

Yearning has a dreadful will,
love's is sadder.
Everything is power, stopping at nothing.

The smell of his hot palms and rugged chest,
his eyes, his testicles moistening
against my nightdress

my man, on Sunday,
this is how I've longed to live:
it's actuality, morning
that your mouth tastes of

the tree-blossoms have woken already, and their babies
are being toted by the wind

Children are
a chronological illusion.

The soul is just prattling by itself
in death's arms.

One and the same heart is caressing itself.

from LIGHT THROUGH OPENING DOORS / RAOTTUVIEN OVIEN VALO (1989)

The grass dreams of rain,
the tree of wind.
Alone in the cantrap of our labyrinth
we crochet locked roses on the lace of fantasy.
                                        We alone
have this soiled face, in our eyes
the simultaneous fever and chill of stars.
We feel our fate: lovely
is the realised dream,
lovelier the unrealised.

the dim gold-edged envelopes
of doors, the groundswells of anticipation, the hair's
rustling curtains:

on a rainy day
I seduce you:

so translucent and heavy the water is
down my mouth my neck my breasts
the hot coins of your pupils.

And love wearies
towards its own goal:
the eyes, vacant, full
ogle the afternoon; in the sky
the clouds gash, and go, and the birds
wear fate's
little black tailcoats.

Perhaps the birds don't
actually die quickly, in mid-spring,
over the ocean,
perhaps they tire into the sun and the clouds' names,
into their tracks rushing horizonwards,
cower in a cliff-hole, on a moss-pad perhaps,

and the wind carries off the last feather
like a rejected dream.